Making Sense of Space

Chandos
Information Professional Series

Series Editor: Ruth Rikowski
(email: Rikowskigr@aol.com)

Chandos' new series of books is aimed at the busy information professional. They have been specially commissioned to provide the reader with an authoritative view of current thinking. They are designed to provide easy-to-read and (most importantly) practical coverage of topics that are of interest to librarians and other information professionals. If you would like a full listing of current and forthcoming titles, please visit www.chandospublishing.com.

New authors: we are always pleased to receive ideas for new titles; if you would like to write a book for Chandos, please contact Dr Glyn Jones on g.jones.2@elsevier.com or telephone +44 (0) 1865 843000.

Making Sense of Space

The design and experience of virtual spaces as a tool for communication

IRYNA KUKSA
AND
MARK CHILDS

ELSEVIER

AMSTERDAM • BOSTON • CAMBRIDGE • HEIDELBERG • LONDON
NEW YORK • OXFORD • PARIS • SAN DIEGO
SAN FRANCISCO • SINGAPORE • SYDNEY • TOKYO
Chandos Publishing is an imprint of Elsevier

CP
CHANDOS
PUBLISHING

Chandos Publishing
Elsevier Limited
The Boulevard
Langford Lane
Kidlington
Oxford OXS 16B
UK
store.elsevier.com/Chandos-Publishing-/IMP_207/

Chandos Publishing is an imprint of Elsevier Limited

Tel: +44 (0) 1865 843000
Fax: +44 (0) 1865 843010
store.elsevier.com

First published in 2014

ISBN: 978-1-84334-740-8 (print)
ISBN: 978-1-78063-406-7 (online)

Chandos Information Professional Series ISSN: 2052-210X (print) and ISSN: 2052-2118 (online)

Library of Congress Control Number: 2014931727

British Library Cataloguing-in-Publication Data.
A catalogue record for this book is available from the British Library.

Typeset by Domex e-Data Pvt. Ltd., India
Transferred to Digital Printing in 2014

Contents

List of figures

Acknowledgements

I would like to thank Professor Jim Davis and James Fair for reading the first draft of this book and for their helpful comments, encouragement and warm words. I am also very grateful to Deborah Tuck who contributed to the case study – 'Exploring the Nottingham Reform Bill Riots through augmented reality' – in Part 2 of the book, and to the Harry Ransom Centre, where the research for the 'Scenography reborn in 3D' case study took place. I thank especially my co-author Dr Mark Childs – not only for his hard work but also for being a very good friend. Finally, I thank Dr Christian Rutz for his interest in my work and for the support he gave me while I was working on this book.

Iryna Kuksa

I would like to thank Professors Jim Davis and Grainne Conole for reading through Parts 3 and 4 of the book and for giving me very timely suggestions on additions. I would also like to thank Graham Lewis and John Carter McKnight for their ideas and conversations about the topics of my part of this book, Anna Peachey for providing me with a place to start and for introducing me to first, second and third places, and above all to Diane Dupres for the many discussions about the last of the connections that made the idea of a 'fourth place' come together. I am also very grateful to all practitioners and academics who contributed to the case studies in Parts 3 and 4 of the book. Finally, thanks are due especially to Dr Iryna Kuksa – for providing me initially with a platform to write, and with whom the back and forth over the content of my sections resulted in the honing of my arguments and improvements in style. In the end it was worth it.

Mark Childs

About the authors

Iryna Kuksa is a research fellow in art and design at Nottingham Trent University in the UK. In her research, Iryna investigates the challenges, and opportunities, encountered by practitioners and educators in using immersive virtual environments and in applying 3D visualization as research methodology. She examines a suite of rapidly-developing communication and computer-visualization techniques, which enable reciprocal exchange between viewers and artefacts and which transform the way in which we experience, learn and co-create our culture.

Iryna is also Reviews Editor for *Scene* (published by Intellect), Senior Visiting Research Fellow at Staffordshire University, and has recently been awarded a Harry Ransom Fellowship to conduct her research on Norman Bel Geddes' theatrical presentations at the University of Texas at Austin. Her broad research interests enable Iryna to make creative and inventive connections between various areas of knowledge, identifying exciting research questions and methodologies. She aspires to continue her research on immersive virtual environments, which are already an important aspect of current teaching and research and which promise enormous future potential for scholars in terms of understanding virtual ecologies and the sustainability of virtual performance spaces. Iryna can be contacted at *iryna.kuksa@ntu.ac.uk*.

Mark Childs is a senior research fellow at Coventry University, a senior researcher at Loughborough University and a visiting fellow at Leicester University. He is also a freelance consultant working within academia. Since 1997 Mark has worked on more than 30 projects involving technology-supported learning – as a researcher, consultant, evaluator, manager and principal investigator at Coventry University, and in previous posts at the Universities of Wolverhampton and Warwick. In 2010, he was awarded a Ph.D. from the University of Warwick for his thesis on 'Learners' experiences in virtual worlds'.

In his freelance work, Mark has been a consultant and evaluator for a range of private and public sector organizations, including Hewlett Packard, the Field Museum of National History in Chicago, Ravensbourne College, the Open University and JISC. His main research focus is the user experience of synchronous communication platforms, with his most recent work including virtual teamworking, online collaboration and peer learning via technology, but particularly learning and performance in virtual worlds and mixed reality. Mark can be contacted at *mark@markchilds.org*.

Introduction

Introduction and rationale for the book

We live in the digital age – the age of seamless communication and interactivity. We inhabit cyberspace (an unlimited, constantly expanding electronic terrain), which correlates with our physical reality, gradually becoming part of it. We use it for saving and storing information, for facilitating knowledge exchange and, importantly, for communicating with one another. Virtual spaces are not simply another way for people to express themselves in the same way they used to do. One might argue that they radically changed human perceptions of the surrounding world and even could be considered as a form of art.

There is little doubt that technological development and its capability to constantly produce new multimedia applications is endless (at least to date). This affects our means of communication and brings a new (quite interactive) quality to our experiences of everyday life, art, history and culture. Interactivity is often referred to as something specific to new media technologies; in reality, however, it is an attribute of any representational media that simply enables a new form of communication. In his 2002 essay, 'Reflections on digital imagery: of mice and men', Paul Willemen defined interactivity as 'a significant feature from classical Chinese poetry to the call-and-response structures of gospel and jazz music, to Surrealism's "exquisite corpses" and to just about all forms of commercial verbal and imaged discourses in which feedback mechanisms have played a determining role for at least a century' (Willemen, 2002: 14). Several years before this statement, back in 1999, Johannes Birringer distinguished the following modes of interaction applicable to digital artistic spaces that are still relevant nowadays. The first mode is a touch-screen interactivity that is widely presented in inter-media exhibitions and video installations with Internet access. The second mode is interactivity that extends deeper into digital space, implying distance and spatial separation; it involves reciprocity and feedback, and can be used in broadcast media. And the third mode represents a conceptual structure of the meeting points and conduits of interactive levels and suggests that interactive digital art is not subject to a particular technological mode, but is the intermixing of analogue and telematic (which is a combination of computers and telecommunications) media. These different modes are not only providing alternative locations for performers, artists and educators to conduct their practice, but they are also raising fundamental questions about the nature of these disciplines. Computer-based media and the variety of platforms they provide are interactive by definition. However, one of the main questions this book investigates is whether these different platforms actually constitute *locations* in the generally accepted meaning of the word, and whether there is a need for us to change our conceptions of what space, place and interaction actually are?

To address the above issues, the authors provide a comprehensive analysis of the use of digital spaces in performance, design, education and cultural heritage – the domains they are most familiar with. Their work with a range of technologies within physical classrooms and virtual worlds is informed by innovative developments in their fields and contributes to the debate about the potential of digital environments and reappraisal of the role of space. The chapters presented in this book are an amalgamation of the authors' observations and reflections on these topics, as well as a critical analysis of their audiences' experiences. Furthermore, the collaborative nature of the authors' work, which has informed this research, has defined its format as a blend of two different forms of a research-led publication. This is a co-authored book with two collaborating (and sometimes competing) voices that created most of the content. In addition, however, some chapters of the book are co-written with other contributors and presented here as case studies, which makes this book a joint endeavour by a multitude of researchers and practitioners. This variety of viewpoints enables the reader to get a clear picture about various theoretical underpinnings that inform the authors' research, to find out about different uses of virtual spaces, and to learn about some of the underlying rationales and debates that facilitate their use.

The structure of the book

As with any study that aims to lay the groundwork for an area of debate, or even to provide a simple introduction to the field which may be unfamiliar to some readers, the process of exploring the topic of this book begins with a definition of terms. This is particularly important when the experiences being discussed are still largely unfamiliar, and where the field is still so nascent that no single specific definition has been adopted by the majority of practitioners. Part 1 lays out some of these definitions, explores conflicting interpretations (where these arise in the literature) and gives an overview of the history of digital environments, their cultural use and applications. This part also provides theoretical and practitioner points of view on how virtual spaces – as a tool for communication, interaction and creativity – could enhance research, practice and learning activities. Iryna Kuksa begins Part 2 by looking into how digital spaces are planned and created through analysing the ways in which virtual reality and other technological applications are placed within design and cultural heritage practices. She scrutinizes the importance of three-dimensional (3D) visualization as a research tool, and discusses the paradigm shifts between traditional interface design and design for virtual environments and the ways that 3D perception is realized within them. Kuksa explores the notion of direction in virtual spaces with a particular focus on digital museums and virtual heritage sites and the importance of seamless knowledge navigation. In Part 3, Mark Childs discusses various interpretations of space that have been employed by numerous writers and researchers, beginning with Heidegger in 1920s and his notion of *Dasein*, as well as our relationship to it. Childs examines such concepts as Huizinga's 'Magic Circle' and Oldenburg's notion of 'Third Space', along with investigating the role that navigation plays in 3D environments. He proposes an extension to Oldenburg's taxonomy of space by introducing a concept of 'fourth space' that describes the common features of theatre in virtual worlds. The variety of notions of space is then applied to discussions about the use of virtual worlds in performance and education, as they relate to specific education case studies in Parts 2 and 3 and to the work of five theatre and performance practitioners in Part 4. These practitioners are each given a voice, and their statements reflect recent and future developments in their fields. Finally, Part 5 – the Conclusion – summarizes these separate themes and merges them, examining the differences and similarities between physical and virtual, and how an analysis of each informs the nature of the other and potentially the future of both.

Part 1
Spaces, presence, realities ...

1

Remediating technology, translating experience, immersing in spaces

Abstract: This first chapter examines the ways in which we use virtual worlds for communication, learning and creative practices, applying two different theoretical approaches to describe the process of adapting spaces from one medium to another. It looks into the history of virtual spaces and the evolution of new media technologies, providing definitions of terms used frequently to describe the digitality of our everyday experiences. Some of these terms have a multitude of definitions or became interchangeable in the literature, leading to some confusion among researchers. Here, we attempt to clarify, explain and, in places, even redefine some of these terms, aiming at establishing a more coherent approach to researching technological evolution and the emergence of virtual spaces.

Key words: cyberspace, virtual reality, new media technologies, telepresence, immediacy, psychological and perceptual immersion, remediation, translation, mixed reality, augmented reality.

A history of virtual spaces and definitions of basic terms

Virtual reality (VR) is a term frequently used in the literature, but to date there is no consensus about how it should be defined. A generally accepted definition of VR is a computer simulation of a real or imaginary system that enables users to perform operations in virtual spaces and shows effects in real time. It is also a part of the global information and communication infrastructure – or cyberspace. 'What is real?' asked the character of Morpheus in the blockbuster movie *The Matrix* (1999, Warner Bros. Pictures). The simple answer would be anything we can explore through our senses. However, our senses can deceive us and something that appears *real* can be *unreal* at the same time. To some extent, the terms *computer technology* and *digital technology* have become interchangeable. *Digitality* emerged as instantaneous communication, global connectivity and ubiquitous media that are in charge of almost every aspect of our everyday experience (Gere, 2002). It refers to the capabilities of a particular technology and the way we think about it, combining both technical and creative components and stimulating further technological evolution. Digital technology produces a vast range of applications and media forms, such as virtual reality, digital film and television, electronic music, computer games and various special effects for the entertainment industry, including theatre. At present, it is so well integrated that it appears almost 'natural' due to its increasing invisibility. In order to understand how our reality has become *digital*, it is necessary to look back into the logic of its progression.

Lev Manovich, one of the leading theorists of digital culture and media art, distinguishes two distinct trajectories in the development of new media. The first one is *representational* technologies, such as film, audio and video magnetic tape, as well as various digital storage formats. The second trajectory is *real-time communication* technologies – telegraph, telephone, telex, television, telepresence and also virtual and augmented realities (AR). The revolutionary advent of the printing press in the fourteenth century was responsible for the first large-scale media transformation, which resulted in a complete change in communicating visual culture. Furthermore, the invention of photography in the nineteenth century – a major scientific and artistic breakthrough – dramatically altered mankind's perception and experience of the world. The emergence of cyberspace, as a digital network, remediated the electric communication means of the past 150 years, including the telegraph and telephone. Jay David Bolter and Richard Grusin, authors of *Remediation: Understanding New Media*, further argue that cyberspace refashions the visual spaces of painting, film and television, and, additionally, such social and historical places as cities and parks, and such *non-places* as theme parks and shopping malls (Bolter and Grusin, 1999). Despite remediation, all aforementioned media organically coexist and evolve together, as well as contribute and relate to each other's content. Each of these spaces is a hybrid of technical, social and economic practices and offers its own path to *immediacy*, with an ability to converge and create something new. Immediacy is often referred to as the absence of a perception that technology is mediating the activity. It is also frequently contrasted with the idea of *hypermediacy*, in which the technology is perceived. In most cases, complete immediacy is the aim of communication technologies; the noticeable presence of technology is often considered as being a perceptual impediment to a complete feeling of connection with the virtual space, or with others within it. Bolter and Grusin claim that at the present level of technological development, the telephone offers the immediacy of the voice, the television promises the immediacy through its real-time monitoring of the world, and, eventually, the computer facilitates the immediacy that comes through the synthesis of 3D graphics, programming and interactivity (ibid.). In this book, immediacy is equated with transparency, where the medium is virtually absent, making the perception of spaces obstruction- and distraction-free. It is also noted, however, that with some creative, performance and also educational activities, the very awareness of the mediating technology is the aim, where participants (or learners) are asked to focus on the technology and explore their understanding of or reaction to it. Hypermediacy aims to problematize, or seek to question, our relationship with technology, while immediacy aims to use technology to maintain or enhance our relationships with others or with the space. The highest form of immediacy occurs in the *interfaceless* types of technology such as VR; however, the majority of experiences lie somewhere along the spectrum of complete immediacy and complete hypermediacy (Dobson, 2009: 2).

In the 1984 novel *Neuromancer*, William Gibson described VR as a fact of our daily experiences and defined ever-growing computer networks as an 'unthinkable complexity – as a cyberspace' (Gibson, 1984: 51). Cyberspace emerged as a computer-generated, navigable infinity that seemingly exists behind the computer screen and is able to connect and separate its users at the same time as they are actively engaged in the networked electronic communication (Kuksa and Childs, 2010). It is a space we can inhabit and also a popular trend across computer culture. Cyberspace has already established itself as a standard in human–computer interfaces and digital networks. It embraces a vast range of 3D digital environments that could have some correlation with the real world or could be completely imaginary, such as, for example, online multi-player computer games and virtual learning hubs. These spaces are interactive, navigable in real time, and are not bound by any physical limitations. The current advances in VR applications include the use of computer imaging, sound and sensory systems, in order to put participants in a direct feedback loop with the technology itself and the world it simulates. Rather than offering an environment in which to simply view and hear, as, for example, in traditional theatre or cinema space, VR attempts to create an experience in which users feel as if they are physically involved in the world represented on all sensory levels. There are various external hardware and visualization systems that make interaction with virtual environments possible and achieve different levels of immersion – an experience that underlies all the interactions within virtual and remote spaces. Interestingly, it has proved very difficult for researchers and writers to define the term *immersion* clearly. There is a general agreement, however, that immersion is not unique to the digital world, because culturally we are long familiar with the idea of becoming 'lost' in a book, theatre play, film or television programme. Janet Murray notes that the derivation of this term comes from the experience of being submerged in water. She states that the practice of being 'transported to an elaborately simulated *place* [author's emphasis] is a sensation of being surrounded by a completely other reality ... that takes over all of our attention, our whole perceptual apparatus' (1997: 98). Matthew Lombard and Theresa Ditton (1997) argue that this feeling (which occurs while, for example, watching a television programme) could be described as being 'more like "somewhere that I visited" rather than "something that I saw"'. Psychological immersion is sometimes referred to as *presence*, which in its turn is occasionally taken as an abbreviation of *telepresence* (Biocca, 1997). For a long time, these concepts have been used interchangeably across the literature, with different authors creating their own distinctions between the terms. For example, some writers define presence as 'the natural perception of an environment' and telepresence as 'the mediated perception of an environment' (Steuer, 1995: 36); while others interpret it as 'a perceptual illusion of nonmediation' with immediacy (as a concept) blurred within this definition (Lombard and Ditton, 1997). Furthermore, Lombard and Ditton identified another aspect of immersion – *perceptual immersion* – the degree to which 'what you see' submerges the perceptual system of the user, enabling them to disregard the medium. Frank Biocca, however, objected to describing technology by the degree to which the senses are engaged through the displays of the interface (or *vividness*) because this 'confuses independent and dependent variables by defining a property of the interface, the computer, in terms of the effect of this property on the user' (1997). This is true, but it is also the fundamental flaw in any discussion about the nature of immersion. The objective design of the technologies does not, in itself, determine the degree to which immersion occurs. Though they may be called 'immersive technologies' (and indeed greater vividness and more interaction contribute to the potential for 'being immersed'), immersion is also dependent on a range of other factors separate from the technology. Blocking out sensory input from the real world, for example, also adds to the sense of psychological immersion, but the perception of our real bodies can disrupt it (Murray and Sixsmith, 1999: 318, 327). Since no concrete definitions exist for exploring the aforementioned ideas, it becomes necessary to delineate them within any text, including this one, as well as to clarify the discussions for the reader.

For the purposes of this book, *psychological immersion* will be defined as the sense of submergence in a space that is not one's immediate physical environment. *Perceptual immersion*, in its turn, will be characterized as the degree to which one's perceptions are dominated by the technology. We will use the word *immediacy* to describe the perception of non-mediation (or, rather, the lack of perception of mediation). We presume that immediacy is not necessarily synonymous with psychological immersion, as it is, from the experiences of the authors, quite possible without the appearance of non-mediation. For example, when we are in the virtual world Second Life, it is apparent that this world is mediated because we can see an interface, pop-up boxes and, in addition, there may be lag or partial rendering. However, we are accustomed to these interferences, so they are not impediments to the sensation of being drawn into that world, which makes psychological immersion possible. We will accept that defining technologies by their impact on the viewer is problematic (taking Biocca's line of argument), but will still employ the term *immersiveness* in the understanding that this is merely an objective measure of the degree of vividness and interactivity of a technology and is not automatically related to greater immersion. Furthermore, we will consider immediacy and immersiveness as being distinct, in that immediacy requires a natural or invisible interface, while immersiveness involves breadth and depth of sensory engagement together with interactivity. Although these concepts both contribute to perceptual immersion, they are not identical. We base this judgement on the cases when the user becomes perceptually immersed while engaged with a high-resolution visual environment with surround sound via a 'visible' computer interface, but still does not possesses full immediacy. In summary, therefore, we have the following arguably distinct categories:

- *Psychological immersion* – the sense of being submerged in the experience of the environment. It occurs, for example, when we watch a television programme and become emotionally involved in the experiences of the characters, or lose track of time when playing a game, to the extent that we become less aware of our surroundings.

- *Perceptual immersion* – the degree to which the technology dominates the senses, and comprised of immediacy (the lack of perception of mediation) and immersiveness (the objective measure of the vividness [or realism] of the technology, and its degree of interactivity). An example of a completely perceptually immersive environment is Cybersphere at the University of Warwick (*https://digital.warwick.ac.uk/Informatics-and-Virtual-Reality/cybersphere.html*). It was designed for a variety of applications, including construction, healthcare, training and simulation, ultimately aiming to overcome the inability of a user to move around the virtual environment in a natural way. This hollow 3.5 metre diameter construction allows the visitors to stand and walk inside it, tracking their movements and adjusting the internal projections in response to them (Fernandes et al., 2003: 142). Cybersphere achieves total perceptual immersion in that it completely surrounds the user, and is totally interfaceless. While contributing to psychological immersion, perceptual immersion is not necessary for it to occur.

One might argue that to date VR (as technology) offers the most fully immersive 3D experience. With the help of various devices, such as head-mounted displays, data gloves or body suits, users can experience computer-generated spaces that appear to respond to their actions. Immersion within virtual environments acts as a replacement of the passive aspect of observing a computer monitor and exists in parallel to our own reality. The level of involvement with virtual spaces could be defined as augmented, partially immersive and fully immersive. The decision process, in which participants distinguish between real, virtual and imagined events, is called *virtual reality monitoring* (Hoffman et al., 2001: 565), where the quality of the involvement very much depends on to what extent participants apply a willing suspension of disbelief – the crux of the idea of VR. The film industry is very good at presenting digital spaces as analogous worlds that exist invisibly, and at the same time with our own reality. Film-makers use various computerized devices including motion capture technology to create an illusion of a direct interaction within cyberspace. These innovative applications project the actors in digital worlds in any chosen shape or costume, simultaneously providing a complete record of actions undertaken. This virtually interfaceless experience of virtual environments is probably the most barrier-free human–computer interaction as yet. Some researchers and developers, however, might argue that at present the emphasis is more on graphical and other presentational aspects of VR, rather than on its capabilities as a medium for communication and knowledge exchange.

Furthermore, the recent widespread use of ubiquitous computing has the potential to bring about a new trend in developing advanced computer applications in ways contrary to those of VR, turning everything into a computer interface. In the context of this book (as proposed by Kuksa, 2007), cyberspace is considered as a digitally-created 'parallel' cultural world that contains an immense number of opportunities for creativity, learning and communication. The notion of VR is interpreted here in a literal way, as a means that enables 3D reconstruction and user–virtual space–user collaboration.

Nowadays, there are a number of virtual worlds available for people to become engaged with creatively, to socialize in, or to become part of a multi-player computer game as, for example, *World of Warcraft*. Very often there is a stand-alone definition for each of these digital spaces. For the purposes of this book, the authors attempted to summarize all of their key attributes in the following statement (as suggested by Childs, 2013: iii; after Bell, 2008: 2):

> Virtual worlds represent a 'synchronous and persistent network of people and computer programs (embodied as avatars and agents), facilitated by networked computers, which uses navigable space to engage the user's belief'.

The word *avatar* in this sense means 'a graphical representation of a user within the environment which is under his or her direct control' (as specified by Allbeck and Badler, 2002: 313). It has been employed in this context since 1986 when it was used by F. Randall Farmer and Chip Morningstar in the first virtual world called *Habitat* (Britt, 2008). Although not a 3D environment, *Habitat* is considered to be a predecessor of VR-style applications. It was a development from MUDs – entirely text-based systems, in which multiple users connected with others in a shared social space, originally referred to as dungeons, but more recently as domains (Turkle, 1995: 180–1). MUDs are spaces with which one can interact through the manipulation of elements stored as objects in the database. These objects encompass the artefacts within the space, the participants in the environment, as well as the rooms, houses and even cities in which they are located (Meyer, 1995: 241). The term *object* in this context means any basic building block of the environment (White, 2001: 131). This added a visual element to the existing types of interaction and therefore constituted a very early, and arguably the first, virtual world. Although the aforementioned visual representations signified a step forward in developing VR, this does not mean that the purely text-based environments were not spatial in construction. Towell and Towell in their essay, 'Presence in text-based networked virtual environments or "MUDS"' (1997), described how a virtual space (which they refer to as a TNVE or text-based networked virtual environment) is created in a MUD through the information, which has been organized in such a manner that the user is presented with a textual representation of a room, in which there could be other people with whom they may 'talk'. Talking, in this context, means using the keyboard to communicate with others, and, likewise, 'hearing' means to see textual communication on a monitor. Typically, TNVEs are compartmentalized into rooms joined by entrances and exits; and this presentation of a virtual space to the user has been referred to as 'imposing a spatial metaphor' (ibid: 590).

The spatial metaphor underpins the entire notion of an online space. The term cyberspace implies an actual location (apart from physical space). For example, addresses on the World Wide Web where information is stored are called web*sites*, documents within a computer are referred to as belonging to folders, and software for file-sharing adopts words from their physical equivalents, such as a 'dropbox' or 'cubby'. But what fundamentally distinguishes them from any other online interaction is that environments such as MUDs and virtual worlds confer a specific location to the *user* within the space. This means that rather than being a disembodied viewer of a website or dropping files into a folder, the user is positioned within the space and the coordinates of that location determine the nature of interaction. In MUDs, for example, by placing an avatar into a room one can communicate with others, and objects become closer or further away as a result of this movement and can only be manipulated within a certain distance. This recreates the proximal lived experience of the physical world within the simulated one, and thereby manufactures a believable and engaging sense of space. Although the perceptual immersion in a MUD is minimal (since there is little sensory engagement) and the immediacy is nominal (since communication is always via a keyboard and the space entered is interpreted by reading words on a screen), the sense of *psychological immersion* dominates.

The number of more visually and technologically advanced (than MUDs) virtual spaces expanded during the 1990s. The use of avatars as a tool for communication has remained a cornerstone of the rationale for these virtual worlds, encouraging much research into the social aspect of interaction (for example, Schroeder's *The Social Life of Avatars* [2002]). Throughout the last ten years, Second Life – a virtual land space, consisting of a few continents and many small islands – dominated much of the social activity and educational practices 'behind the computer screen'. It was launched in 2003 by Linden Lab and is still hosted on their servers. Second Life land can be bought for a variety of purposes by any registered user and its residents can create their own objects within the space by means of adding together basic geometric shapes known as prims (short for primitives). An active economy exists in there, allowing the users (represented by avatars inworld) to buy and sell these objects using the currency of Linden dollars, which can be exchanged for US dollars (the exchange rate is about 300 Linden dollars to one US dollar). In 2010 and 2011, a separate Teen Second Life (for 13- to 18-year-olds) was closed and the subsidy for many educational institutions represented there was temporarily rescinded. This development led to many educators leaving Second Life, in order to explore other platforms such as OpenSim. Although similar to Second Life from a technological viewpoint (and compliant with the Second Life viewer), OpenSim can be hosted on an institution's own server without the involvement of the 'middleman' (i.e., Linden Lab).

Spaces in virtual and augmented reality: an explanation of the concept of telepresence and mixed reality

Telepresence as a term was used first by Marvin Minsky in 1980 to describe the experience of the operator of remotely located devices. Choosing the popular science magazine *Omni* to reach a wider readership than that of a technical journal, Minsky laid out the timescale, cost and potential applications of this technology. This publication had a seminal influence on the field and the term telepresence has since been adopted (and continuously redefined) by many researchers concerned with the experience of interacting remotely. According to Bolter and Grusin (1999), telepresence refashions the monitoring function of broadcast television and closed-circuit video, by using video signals and computer graphics to place its users at a distant or inaccessible location. This ability, for instance, is significant for the world of education. It allows, for example, a virtual teacher to be present as a holographic image in front of the geographically remote students to conduct a real-time lecture. Telepresence differs from video conferencing in the way that it provides more natural communication, establishing perfect eye contact between its users, which is achievable by employing specific optically-embedded camera technologies. By contrast, video conferencing is typically a two-way video system, with cameras usually placed on the top of the monitor, making participants look at each other's images instead of the cameras. AR employs techniques similar to telepresence by placing computer graphics or video in front of the participants. The AR users can see the real and virtual world simultaneously, meaning that instead of blocking the real environment, the computer 'overwrites' and comments on what a spectator sees. The main difference between telepresence and AR is that AR offers a *hypermediated* experience where its users are very much aware of computer graphics as a medium, while, for example, during the telepresence lecture, students potentially could forget that the knowledge delivery happens through a holographic image of a real teacher. In contrast to telepresence and AR, VR acts as a graphics engine. Although it still remains relatively dependent on previous technological applications, VR represents the next level in the creation of a 'transparent' medium. Together with AR, VR has a great potential to enhance and even completely transform any cultural, heritage or theatrical space. The main difference between the two, however, is that whereas VR aims to replace the real world, AR attempts to supplement it. Interestingly, the key characteristic of collaborative AR would be *virtuality* that allows the objects, which do not exist in the real world, to be viewed and examined in a computer-generated environment. This enables multiple participants to control their own independent viewpoints, in order to see each other, cooperate in a natural way, and, overall, to avoid a feeling of social exclusion. In addition, the displayed data can vary from viewer to viewer, which intensifies face-to-face interaction and allows AR users to collaborate seamlessly and simultaneously with both virtual and real environments. Nowadays, there are a number of smartphone AR applications ranging from browsers (for example, Wikitude World Browser and Layar) that provide relevant-to-the-user geographical information displayed on a mobile phone screen as they walk, to AR fitting rooms – an innovation for shoppers, who can try on a great variety of outfits before completing a purchase.

Making communication in virtual worlds more *natural* has always been the ultimate goal for any VR developer through various ways of merging virtual and real spaces. In 1994, Paul Milgram and his colleague Haruo Takemura introduced the Reality–Virtuality Continuum (Figure 1.1). Here, real and virtual environments are referred to as the *continuum*, as opposed to an antithesis. One end of the continuum contains a real

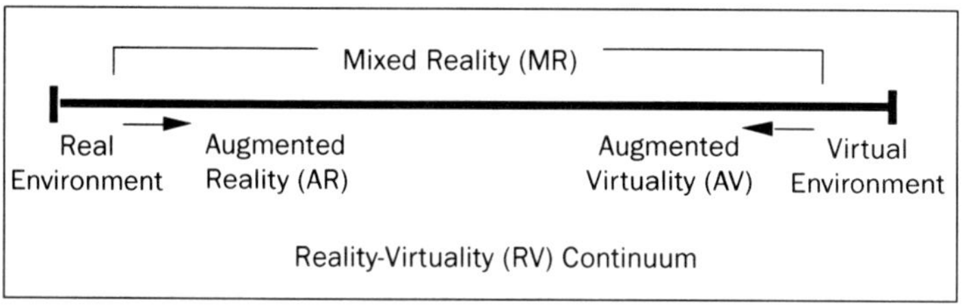

Figure 1.1 **Reality–Virtuality Continuum**

Source: published in *SPIE* Vol. 2351, Telemanipulator and Telepresence Technologies, 1994. Reproduced with permission of Professor Paul Milgram

environment that consists only of real objects and can be viewed directly in person, or through some kind of display. By contrast, the other extreme consists solely of virtual environments, such as monitor-based or immersive computer graphic simulations. AR here pertains to any environment which is simply enhanced by means of computer graphics, but otherwise is completely real. And, eventually, augmented *virtuality* comprises the enhancement of completely virtual environments with real images and objects. Within this framework, mixed reality (MR) refers to 'the class of all displays in which there is some kind of combination of real and virtual environments' (Milgram and Drascic, 1997: 1).

More than ten years ago, Mark Billinghurst stated that MR systems could be divided into two major groups: *video see-through* and *optical see-through* mixed reality (Billinghurst and Kato, 1999). This division depends on the relative proportions of display methods used. While employing video MR, the interaction with the real world is slightly unnatural. It happens because all virtual objects are superimposed on a live video image of a real environment and displayed back into the user's eyes. This image is captured by the camera attached to a head mounted display (HMD), the viewpoint of which is offset from the user's own, so that the image it produces is not stereographic. The main advantage of this system, however, is relatively easy implementation. In contrast to video MR, the second system shows virtual objects directly in the real world by using see-through displays. Virtual images are stereoscopic and can be generated in such a way that the interaction with them seems to be natural, and the user sees the real world directly. This makes optical see through displays more reliable for the simultaneous viewing of virtual and real environments without distortion of the images.

Cultural use of cyberspace – paradigms of digital reality

Such fields as education, art and design, entertainment, scientific research, communication and information studies, as well as marketing and advertising, have been widely employing technology-led applications for a decade at the very least. Collaborative virtual environments (CVEs), for example, have been used for communication but also for educational activities since 1987, beginning with the development of the SIMNET virtual system (Joslin et al., 2004: 28), which served as a platform for real-time distributed combat simulation by the US military. Indeed, computer-based simulations have been around for many years, allowing users to improve their physical skills in non-risk digital environments (for example, fighter-jet pilot training), but also to attend multimedia exhibitions and virtual art displays. Avatar-inhabited virtual communities have always been very popular for communication and socializing, but they are also used for staging virtual theatre performances, for organizing conferences and seminars, and as a trial space for new product launches (allowing their visualization and testing prior to implementation or after complete demolition). The examples here might include 3D reconstructions of ancient buildings, historical stages and sets based on archaeological and visual evidence. This virtual modelling approach enables researchers to investigate various objects, which, for instance, may be either too large or too small in scale to be explored in real life, or which were lost in the past or do not yet actually exist. These platforms for conceptual navigation, creativity and historical reconstruction could be linked to numerous digital resources, including information points and displays, virtual libraries and databases, electronic books and visualization products for users to utilize.

In 2003, Oliver Grau identified three paradigms of after-2000 artistic practices:

1. the paradigm of illusion;
2. resemblance to life; and
3. presence in other places.

The last of these is the principal focus of this book. A good example here would be the work of Stelarc – a performer and artist who, through his art practice, is exploring the extremes of physical and transhumanist expression (he is also one of the contributors to this book). Stelarc examines performance in the new realm of virtual worlds, focusing on how they alter the relationship between 'the artist' and 'the body'. He performs in mixed realities, using AR to bring his inworld performances into the real world (Figure 1.2). Furthermore, he embodies his own physical form within virtual spaces and performs as an avatar in Second Life. This is only the latest manifestation of a decades-long career exploring the nature of humanity, and how this alters (and is defined by) our relationship with technology. As he says in his contribution to Part 4 of this book: 'I think it's not meaningful to imagine that there's an intrinsic human and that we're somehow going towards an alien "other". What it means to be human in fact is to become that alien other.'

Modern audiences are spoiled by the sophisticated technological effects used in contemporary communication and entertainment media, the film industry and theatre. Films and sometimes plays are now expected to provide a high level of special effects for the sake of amusement. It is necessary to emphasize, however, that theatrical reality, as opposed to the cinematograph (especially Hollywood blockbusters) and television, goes far beyond simply using any technology *per se*. Throughout theatre history, there have been numerous attempts to use technological capacity on stage to its very maximum. Very often these endeavours were highly appreciated by audience members, but also widely criticized by contemporary critics, accusing theatres of eliminating theatricality for the sake of technology. Christopher Baugh (2005), for example, highlights the career of the stage designer Bruce 'Sensation' Smith at Drury Lane Theatre in London, who used hydraulic stage machinery widely in the early 1900s for a series of sensation melodramas. He argues that the 'classic plays of antiquity and of Shakespeare were presented as little more than glittering *tableaux vivants*, with the words of the text functioning as little more than "sub-titles" to animated pictures' (ibid.: 181). Soon after, the twentieth century modernity post-modernity paradigm shift also warmly welcomed new technologies, seeing them as a major breakthrough to new art forms and practices. This shift gave birth to numerous dramatically and technologically sophisticated productions possessing the 'wow factor' – the trend which remains very much alive within contemporary theatre and cinematographic practices. Indeed, the audience's 'thirst' for being entertained through spectacular effects has been in existence for centuries, encouraging creative practitioners to experiment heavily with new techno-tools. Some technology critics argue that this fascination with technology causes a shift towards the aesthetics of a computer model, rather than the appropriateness of the design concept. This is a

Figure 1.2 **Stelarc performing in the *Extract/Insert* installation in the Herbert Art Gallery, Coventry, UK, 2012**

Source: Reproduced with permission of Dena de Rougemont

strong statement and sometimes it might be the case, but, undoubtedly, there are also numerous advantages in employing technology as a design partner. It simplifies editing work, in which various scanned images and other visual objects are easily included and preserved at any point during the creative process. Furthermore, the integration of light, animation and kinetic elements enhances the storyboard and makes it look realistic. The rendered models are navigable, can be viewed from any direction, and can be easily transported via email or file hosting services, facilitating communication between specialists involved in the production. This possibility of working in digital space provides creative inspiration and makes workflow more efficient, by moving easily between graphic programs, digital models and schematic outputs. On the other hand, however, even specialized software is not always able to solve every technical design issue, and it can also be expensive and difficult to learn. In addition, it is impossible to interact physically with a computer model, and, frankly, physical space will never look quite the same as its computer generated prototype. Some professionals also argue that the ability to make endless revisions is another big disadvantage of computer-based design projects, because it might greatly affect any intended outcomes by leaving the project in a constantly unfinished state. This is a very important issue, which will be further investigated in some of the following chapters.

There are a number of pros and cons outlined above, but despite existing criticism virtual spaces are an integral part of the contemporary events industry landscape and they do assist creative practitioners throughout different stages of concept visualization and implementation. The Theatrebase project is a good example of how virtual worlds could inform the practice of set designers. This project is a collaboration led by Daden Limited (a company that provides design and support in the use of virtual worlds and virtual agents), the Birmingham Royal Ballet and Birmingham Hippodrome theatre, together with the Serious Games Institute based at Coventry University. Much of the design work for Theatrebase was conducted by Ian Upton (another of the contributors to this book). The goal of the project was to test the suitability of virtual worlds and serious games technology in supporting the backstage and technical management of large theatre productions. Although usually set designers develop smaller (1:25 scale) versions of the sets from cardboard, called model boxes, to test out visually and practically how the set elements fit together on a particular theatre stage, these are often designed around an optimal viewing position. Putting sample sets within a full recreation of the Birmingham Hippodrome, complete with a full auditorium modelled in Second Life, enables the set to be viewed from any specific seat in the theatre (Figure 1.3) and by anyone with Internet access, simply by logging on to Second Life.

This approach creates marketing opportunities for taking a production on tour, as well as enabling a standard 'off the peg' modification for placing the set on a smaller stage. Furthermore, by modelling a variety of theatres it would also be possible to modify set designs in advance, in order to fit them on specific stages and around the loading capacity of flybars, and also for theatre managers and potential audience members to see them *in situ*. This opportunity to test various set-ups before the production is actually on tour would greatly reduce the time and labour spent on rebuilding the sets on-site. Another aspect of the Theatrebase project was the recreation of the backstage area to model the path that the props make from the loading bay to the stage. This enables any obstructions (such as tight corners or protruding ducts) to be taken into account while building the set, as well as for load plans (how set elements fit together in the containers for transportation) to be optimized. Furthermore, virtual models of theatre spaces could if necessary include metadata elements about the set and props such as weight, fragility and

Figure 1.3 View of the Birmingham Hippodrome stage from the auditorium

Source: Reproduced with permission of Daden Limited

specific health and safety information about their installation, which could be updated when needed. Theatrebase revealed much about the relationship between the actual space and its physical and virtual set models. It became apparent early on in the course of the project that the set designers would not change their practice of creating physical models of the sets, because the act of creation for them is a tactile experience. The production process of the virtual space was therefore altered to complement, rather than replace, these physical prototypes. The complete model boxes were created first, and then the physical elements were scanned and used for generating their virtual counterparts. This change in procedure serendipitously led to the idea of reusing the existing archives (collections of model boxes from the decades of previous productions) and recreating the company's past within the virtual world. This opened up the potential application of the project to theatre history research and education.

Remediation and translation: the different theoretical approaches adopted in this book

This book has adopted two theoretical approaches to investigate the technological evolution and emergence of virtual spaces. The first, which has already been discussed above, is a theory of remediation developed by Jay David Bolter and Richard Grusin in 1999. This theory challenged the assumption adopted by many media theorists in the late 1990s that the aesthetics and cultural principles of digital technologies should be treated completely separately from any earlier media. The term *remediation* is used in this book to describe the convergence of different types of media, the absorption of one medium by another, and also to explain the assimilation of new knowledge delivered and experiences encouraged by new technological means. Coming together, each of these technologies is immersed in the others in a way that minimizes the discontinuities between them. However, this does not mean that the older medium is entirely wiped out. On the contrary, the new medium is still dependent on the older one in various ways, which from time to time is not acknowledged.

The use of the word *translation* in Part 3 to describe the process of adapting spaces from one medium to another differs more from a terminology viewpoint rather than a theoretical approach. The rationale for adopting this term is partly an attempt to use a more generic word, but also to co-opt many of the ideas within translation theory and apply these to the work considered here. Translation is in essence a recodification – from the code of the original language to that of the target language (Frawley, 2000: 252) – the intention of which is to perform 'complete interpretive resemblance' (Smith, 2002: 110). For this to be achieved, complete synonymy between the two codes is required, which is not (in practice) what normally exists between two languages. The structural differences between languages mean that 'it is not possible to reproduce the linguistic properties of one language in another. However, it is often possible to identify the communicative clues of the source text and formulate receptor language equivalents that serve the same communicative function' (ibid.: 110–11). This process is analogous to the practice of identifying the affordances of one medium and adapting an artefact or narrative (or in fact a piece of art) to another when moving across media and making the best use of it. Indeed, it is the extent to which narratives adjust to the different modalities that exist in different media that determines the success of their becoming transmedia (Jenkins, 2011). The process of abstraction of meaning also needs to be undertaken by the translator when analysing the source of a narrative, in order for it to be re-coded into the target (or receptor) language (Wu and Xu, 2011: 397). Similarly, when we move from one medium to another (or in the case of the work here, from one reality to another), the re-codification forces the practitioner to consider what are the essential meanings and value of an object, artefact, narrative, or indeed the space that is to be translated to this target or receptor reality. This process of abstraction can be a fascinating and revealing experience in itself, and is often explored by translation theorists who are also concerned with the choices between direct translation (complete interpretive resemblance) and indirect translation (adequate resemblance). The result of direct translation 'should create the impression of reading the receptor language in the source context' (Smith, 2002: 111), meaning that readers can draw all the meaning embedded within the text from the communicative clues of the language in which they are reading it. This may have the advantage of accuracy (and immediacy), but may limit the sources that can be translated to those that have exact synonyms across the two codes (languages). Indirect translation 'aims to convey only those assumptions of the original text that are deemed relevant to the target audience' (ibid.: 110, 112).

Indirect translation can also supplement the communicative clues that are not available from the context of the source language by providing additional background. For example, the endnote that explains the full nuances of the source phrase 'ungeheuren Ungeziefer' in the opening sentence of Franz Kafka's *The Metamorphosis* (Kafka, 1915; translated by Corngold, 1972: 3) means far more than 'monstrous vermin' when read by a Jewish German-speaker living in Prague in the early twentieth century, than when translated for an English speaker a century later (ibid.: 66). This means that this phrase can only exist as an indirect translation, which from an educational point of view is perfectly acceptable. Trying to explain the connotations of 'ungeheuren Ungeziefer' is not only an opportunity to reveal much about the source language and culture, but is also a good example of the relative values of hypermediacy and immediacy. By pointing the reader to an endnote in a book the immersion in the narrative is disrupted and the artificial nature of the experience is made explicit. Hypermediacy is therefore increased as the reader is made aware of the structure of the text; however, the potential for engagement with the meaning of the narrative is enhanced. This has parallels in many educational scenarios that take place in virtual worlds – where the choices are between *replication*, when a physical world is replicated exactly (a direct translation), and *simulation*, where only the aspects that are relevant are converted (often in a rather symbolic manner) to the virtual (an indirect translation).

If we compare the move from the physical to the virtual to the change of text from one language to another, then the issue of translation raises certain questions. If we see this transfer as a recodification, then the translation can never be perfect, since the 'codes' of the physical are so different from the virtual. Where there is a mismatch between these 'codes', then the alternative is to identify the elements of one reality that form the same communicative function in the other.

Conclusion

In this chapter the authors have discussed virtual spaces, which remediate physical cultural environments and are being increasingly used for a variety of purposes. We have observed that very few studies have been able to address a selection of issues connected to the use of virtual spaces. For example, there is a necessity to explore the aesthetic consequences of employing a computer as an active contributor to the creative process (or even redefine what the aesthetics of virtual worlds are). The problem here is that it is difficult to control, for example, the work of art placed in virtual space from how it was created to how it will be or should be perceived by the audience. The term original is foreign to a computer, thus it is not surprising that it is necessary to classify, catalogue and also preserve artefacts, performances and characters once they are translated in digital language. Indeed, every medium and media event is integrated within social and economic environments and cannot exist or work in isolation. This, however, raises such questions as whether and how the copyright conventions will be changed in the context of the digital realm, in order to regulate virtual culture – an issue that remains largely unresolved even nowadays. We are tempted and often encouraged to visit and inhabit virtual spaces, in order to develop new business ideas and artistic practice, to learn and to socialize. The question is whether these activities should be monitored or, on the contrary, whether there should be no censorship so that creativity and entrepreneurialism might flourish. Another important question is how this rapid remediation of the world around us affects our 'selves', transforming cultural identities and a sense of belonging. It is obvious that pure preoccupation with virtual spaces – without attempting to explore new ways of employing this technology for creating something new – appears rather paradoxical. At present, there are a number of online galleries, for example, which offer their viewers a closer look at the images displayed in the actual exhibition space, using their home computers or even organizing art displays taking place only in a virtual space. Bearing in mind these developments, it is hardly surprising that the culture of the modern period with its innovative and interactive dynamism could be regarded as *virtual*. We are surrounded by computer-generated spaces which are very diverse and serve various purposes, meaning that the remediation of the world around us continues and quite possibly will never end. One might argue that cyberspace is an ultimate cultural and communication medium and, indeed, it probably is to date. However, the question – which cannot be answered quite yet – is for how long?

Part 2
Creating virtual spaces

2

Virtual spaces – 'work-in-progress': software, devices and design principles

Abstract: This chapter outlines how various devises are used for the interpretation of our activities into digital data and discusses the paradigm shifts between traditional interface design and design for virtual environments. It explores various technology applications and software applicable to creating, preserving and maintaining virtual spaces, raising the issue of their sustainability. Furthermore, the chapter touches upon the platforms (present and future) we use for generating and managing online content, navigating digital spaces and personifying computer software processes. It discusses a set of design principles crucial for generating educational and cultural activities in virtual worlds and for the research into and dissemination of cultural heritage via computer-based visualization.

Key words: computer aided design, universal design principles, Web 2.0, 3.0 and 4.0 technologies, London Charter, paradata, knowledge navigation.

> The question is not whether digital worlds will change the real world. The question is whether the real world is ready.
>
> (Ondrejka, 2005: 22)

Morton Heilig, a cinematographer of the 1950s, predicted some time ago that the interaction between humans and technology would involve not only senses of sight and sound but also taste, touch and smell. Fourteen years later, in 1964, Marshal McLuhan elaborated on this prediction: '[R]apidly, we approach the final phase of the extensions of man – the technological simulation of consciousness, when the creative process of knowing will be collectively and corporately extended to the whole of human society, much as we have already extended our senses and our nerves by the various media' (McLuhan, 1964: 3–4). Indeed, we enhance our senses by employing virtual and augmented realities and 3D visualizations of places and characters in film-making, military training and medical simulations. We interact with our 'smart' TVs and 'smart' phones on a daily basis, we talk to our 'smart' sat navs and we exercise with 'smart' virtual trainers. Interestingly, all these interactions happen via a screen, an interface or, as some researchers might argue, a barrier to seamless communication. Yehuda E. Kalay added to this observation, stating that 'communication is a process that looks at information from the outside: even though the observer can interact with the information, s/he is not part of it. The computer screen, much like the printed page of a book, stands for a separation from the information, rather than a connection with it' (2004: 199). To overcome this partition, ideally, there should not be any visible and easily recognizable on-screen navigation tools – such as scroll bars, windows or icons – to prevent users from being distracted by the technology and be immediately connected with the content. As discussed previously, just as software developers worked hard to make digital technology transparent and a physical interface 'interfaceless', so users are no longer aware of being face-to-face with a digital medium. Very often, however, participants are used to such intrusions and are not dramatically affected by them, feeling immersed in the experience. There is nothing new in this disagreement among researchers about how 'transparent' the interface should be. Almost fifty years ago, McLuhan defined television as a 'cold' medium (mainly due to the relatively small frame of a TV screen) which prevents the viewer from experiencing the same strength of emotions as, for example, they would while watching a big screen film. Therefore, he referred to a movie theatre as a 'warm' medium despite the fact that both of these media use similar visual display. VR takes the idea of a 'screen' to the next level, revolutionizing the use of television and computer technologies and facilitating cooperative communication in shared 3D spaces. One of the main goals of this technology, which distinguishes it from other media, is to promote natural interaction with and among its users, similar to that in a physical environment.

Since the early 1990s, computer scientists have recognized several paradigm shifts between traditional interface design and design for virtual environments. For example, William Bricken from the Human Interface Technology Laboratory at the University of Washington points out that the first major change happened when the advent of new technological devices enabled their users to 'walk through' the screen surface into inclusive virtual worlds. This innovation was a major technological breakthrough that irreversibly transformed the participant–digital-space relationship. The computer interface with its functionally organized on-screen data enabled 'inclusion' of the users in the computer-generated environments and empowered their direct interaction with various forms of information. The second paradigm shift took place when digital spaces became adapted to natural human behaviour within them. Despite this adaptation, however, some training of participants prior to entry into cyberspace is still desirable and often necessary (this will be discussed further in Part 3). Another important paradigm shift happened with the transformation of virtual world users into active agents capable of generating their own applications and, by doing so, co-creating the matrix of a virtual world. And, finally, the latest change to date was conditioned by the invention of *acoustigraphic* environments, where all movements of the participants involved in a VR experience are multimodal or, to be more precise, can be coordinated with visual representations, as well as with ambient and localized sound. The role of sound within virtual worlds is very important for the psychological assessment and the internal mapping of computer-generated spaces. It gives greater dimension to them and supports the participant's sense of place. VR is a data environment, where interaction between the system and its users happens on different levels of communication with various levels of intensity. This study, however, is mostly concerned with analysing the visual qualities of virtual worlds and the ability of VR applications to help in realizing one of the fundamental objectives in the design process – 3D perception.

There is little doubt that virtual reality modelling is becoming more and more realistic, with the entertainment industry driving its progress. Indeed, 3D graphics have had a revolutionary impact on image production over the last decade. The type of software used for the creation of immersive virtual spaces is a hybrid between CAD (computer aided design, computer aassisted design or computer assisted drafting) and paint programs, offering a combination of vector-based geometry and pixel-based painting. This combination ensures the necessary degree of realism in the final draft, which is reflected in the accuracy of the properties assigned to the objects' surfaces and the lighting effects upon them. Computer programs for CAD are commonly employed by engineers and architects for improving their technical skills and producing precise drafts and plans. This type of software allows the presentation of complex and easily redrawn images and also enables the users to develop their visual projects more accurately. It should be borne in mind, however, that there will always be limits to the realism of digital spaces, objects and characters. Currently, a number of computer scientists (for example Goel et al., 2012) focus their studies on 'intelligent' and 'knowledge-based' CAD systems that deploy artificial intelligence techniques and are concerned with communication and knowledge sharing to promote collaboration and creativity among designers and engineers. Computational systems developed under the influence of new media technologies certainly advanced the management of the design and construction process; however, they have not fully succeeded in making the most of the innovative aspects of information technology. Despite the fact that they solved controlled data management, greatly improving the efficiency of the process, computational technologies also promoted the '"symmetry of ignorance" – the inability of one professional to understand [and communicate] the needs and responsibilities of other professionals' (Kalay, 2006: 361). This happened mainly because such qualitative implications of information technology as its ability to accommodate the individuality and fluent nature of the creative design process were overlooked by the developers. There are platforms, however, that to a certain degree succeeded in promoting communication in digital spaces. In the field of higher education, for instance, there are a number of studies (a recent example being Timmis, 2011) that investigate instant messaging as a means (or tool) of peer-to-peer communication in the process of learning as a social activity. Using this technology implies 'continual multitasking across formal and informal settings and boundaries' (Timmis, 2011: 4), which could either distract learners from the study process or, on the contrary, become a learning support tool. It was established in Chapter 1 that Second Life has also been used extensively for developing new educational approaches and for implementing new learning techniques. However, in 2010, David Kurt Herold noted that: '[T]he focus of many educational sites in Second Life seems to be the creativity of the lecturer or educational support staff, rather than the support of teaching and learning activities involving students dealing with educational challenges in the physical world or in blended learning environments' (Herold, 2010: 792). He further argues that 'there is no conclusive evidence that the environment as such has a huge impact on the teaching and learning process, and the educational use of Second Life should be planned accordingly, by integrating it into a blended learning plan' (ibid.: 797). Indeed, more research is still needed on the benefits of using virtual worlds for meeting pre-set learning goals; however, the process of setting such educational targets should be informed by the available technological platforms that could be used for their delivery.

There are a number of software packages that allow users to create, view, navigate and explore digital spaces socially. Web 2.0 technologies, such as wikis and social networking, not only facilitate shared activities and help to build connections between users via employing graph algorithms and collaborative filtering systems, but also allow them to generate and manage online content at the same time. Some software developers such as Nova Spivack (founder of Radar Networks) predict that Web 3.0 (or the 'Semantic Web' as defined by John Markoff) will enable 'machine-facilitated understanding of information in order to provide a more productive and intuitive user experience ... Web 3.0 will be more connected, open, and intelligent, with Semantic Web technologies, distributed databases, natural language processing, machine learning, machine reasoning, and autonomous agents' (Spivack, 2006). This 'intelligent' web promises to automate the search, collection and analysis of digital data and even to introduce 3D web browsers. These new platforms, which hopefully will be developed in the near future, will once again enhance (or change) the way we communicate with each other; however, it is necessary to remember that despite the technology used the overall success and comfort of the participant–digital-space interaction depends chiefly on how well this space is designed. There are certain principles each designer should have knowledge of, regardless of the area of expertise, in order to accommodate existing demands and to communicate a design concept clearly to the user. In 1998, the Center for Universal Design at North Carolina State University identified a set of the most important principles for guiding the design process, some of which are explained below:

- *Equitable use* – this means that design should be useful and marketable to people with diverse abilities.
- *Flexibility in use* – this implies that design should accommodate a wide range of individual preferences and abilities.
- *Simple and intuitive use* – this suggests that design should be easy to understand, regardless of the user's experience, knowledge, language skills or current concentration level.
- *Perceptible information* – this means that design should communicate necessary information effectively to the users, regardless of ambient conditions or the user's sensory abilities.
- *Error tolerance* – this suggests that design should minimize hazards and the adverse consequences of accidental or unintended actions.

- *Low physical effort* – this implies that design can be used effectively and comfortably and with a minimum of fatigue.
- *Size and space for approach and use* – this means that appropriate size and space are provided for approach, reach, manipulation and use regardless of the user's body size, posture or mobility.

Adapted from Story (1998)

Obviously design processes vary depending on the discipline. However, the above principles are by definition 'universal' and should also be considered when designing digital spaces. This is particularly important because of the use of numerous devices for the interpretation of participant activities into digital data. Indeed, the illusion of being fully immersed in a virtual world can be enhanced by various visual and non-visual technologies. A wide range of hardware, such as projectors, table-tops and ordinary desktops, is specifically designed for viewing computer-generated environments. Projections can be applied onto large concave screens (similar to those used in IMAX theatres) in front of the users or within their walking route. Various devices including HMDs, data gloves and body sensors serve to deliver participants' feedback while interacting in virtual spaces. The head-referenced viewing, typical for immersive VR, provides a natural interface for navigation in a 3D environment, and allows the user to look around, walk around and fly through the scenery. This stereoscopic capability to view virtual worlds, which are perceived in full scale and relate fully to human body size, enhances the perception of depth and the sense of space. Computer games are a good example of the adoption of various navigation techniques to help players to locate themselves within the game environment, including those used in film, when the director is in control of every change of scene and shows the viewer various points of view across the unfolding action. This allows the participant to have an overview of the settings, prioritize what to see and chose a direction to explore the space, while also driving their curiosity. To design such spaces, the Quest3D real-time development engine is normally used. It is based on Microsoft's DirectX (the core Windows technology that drives high-speed multimedia) and is 'a hierarchal node based visual programming system that allows developers with limited programming experience to connect pre-coded function blocks together to rapidly create interactive virtual environments' (Tuck et al., 2009: 1378). Indeed, the notion of direction is an important one while navigating digital spaces. There are, however, some differences in how the user explores them. Second Life, for example, allows for more user input and creativity in comparison to a traditional computer game where participants are penalized if they deviate from expected (pre-programmed) behaviour. Furthermore, virtual heritage environments (VHEs) are structured in a way that enables a seamless, obstruction-free navigation, giving users a feeling that they choose their own path within a virtual historical site. There, the user is not searching for a particular goal to be taken to the next level, but simply 'wayfinding' (Darken and Sibert, 1993) in an immersive environment and learning about the history of the site.

According to Ibanez and Delgado-Mata there are three crucial aspects to be borne in mind when designing interactive virtual environments for any purpose, but particularly for cultural heritage sites: the representation of virtual spaces, navigation support, and addition of life to the environments (2011: 279). In terms of representation, the construction of virtual spaces must include semantic information about the environment in order to make it more interactive. Ibanez and Delgado-Mata suggest using automatic and semi-automatic annotations for this purpose, mainly because contemporary Internet users are accustomed to social commentaries online and these techniques could be highly beneficial for virtual communities. This approach to information delivery in digital spaces is also used for creating virtual museum exhibitions – both on the web or as part of the real display. A group of researchers based at Aristotle University of Thessaloniki in Greece and Coventry University in the UK argue that 'in the 1980s, museums influenced by the New Museology began to change the way they conveyed the context information of the exhibits to the wider public. There was a shift in the museology concept towards considering that the context of a cultural artefact was more important than the item itself' (Styliani et al., 2009: 520–1). To address the demands of new media savvy audiences, virtual exhibition spaces are being designed, enhancing the experience of museum displays and making them more accessible. Styliani et al. (2009) further argue that several of the most characteristic methods and tools currently used for generating virtual museum exhibitions are:

- *Imaging technology* – 'Russian doll' imaging architecture, which gives the user scalability and interactivity opportunities – multiple resolutions of an image are stored in a single file and make it possible to progressively transmit an image. Most popular file formats adopted by cultural institutions are JPEG2000 and FlashPix.
- *Web3D exhibitions* – offers tools such as VRML and increasingly X3D to be used for creating an interactive virtual museum.

Such powerful technologies as OpenSceneGraph (an open source, multi-platform, high-performance 3D graphics toolkit) and a variety of 3D game engines (including serious gaming applications for collaborative use of 3D spaces) are also used in museum environments. Two major drawbacks of this platform are that it requires advanced programming skills, in order to design and implement custom applications, and it doesn't have support for mobile devices – at least not yet.

- *Augmented reality exhibitions* – virtual information (usually 3D objects) is overplayed upon video frames captured by a camera, giving viewers an impression that a virtual artefact exists in the physical world. The augmentation of the real-world environment could lead to a more intuitive access to museum information and enhance its impact on visitors.
- *Haptics* – this platform allows visitors to feel virtual artefacts, simulating the sense of touch. In addition, there is an array of location-aware, multimedia handheld devices and personal digital assistants (PDAs) which are used by various museums and cultural heritage sites (ibid.: 521–4).

It is difficult to say how many virtual exhibition spaces and digital museums are out there – maybe thousands or even tens of thousands. Some of them, however, are unfortunately not sustainable and/or lack clarity. Often, the numerous attempts to exploit the entire graphical capacity of cyberspace lead to an emphasis on the 'wow' factor in creative projects and to the neglect of work on meaningful substance. Richard Beacham elaborated on the above point, stating:

> [W]e are all aware how easily – and how often – some practitioners, including, it must be said, from time to time even established and reputable scholars, have been tempted by the publicity and hype of 'Virtual Reality' as an element of popular culture, to slip into what might be called the 'B.T. Barnum' syndrome, in which scholarship takes second place to showmanship. Models are produced and launched with media hype, articles in the press, and the like, and, in the process, too often questions of accuracy and the scholarly basis for such models are displaced by the undeniably compelling 'magic' of them. In the long run, although such dubious scholarship may draw attention (and even vital findings) to those creating the models, ultimately it carries the risk of discrediting the integrity of

> the research-based process which must be fundamental if such 3-D models are to be perceived and taken seriously by scholars as the extraordinarily valuable 'publications' they undoubtedly have the potential to be.
>
> (Beacham, 2011: 50)

This statement introduced London Charter – the initiative which seeks to establish 3D visualization as an intellectually robust, reliable and rigorous research methodology, and which serves to document historical artefacts in a sustainable and accessible manner. London Charter proposed six key principles applicable to the research or dissemination of cultural heritage, using computer-based visualization. The first principle is the implementation of relevant guidelines (developed by London Charter) by any organization or community of practice concerned with using 3D visualization for historical research at all stages of project development and dissemination of findings. The second principle stipulates that 'computer visualization should normally be used only when it is the most appropriate available method for the purpose' (*http://www.londoncharter.org/*). The third principle explains that relevant research sources (digital and non-digital information used for creating computer-based visualization) should be identified and evaluated in a structured and documented way. The fourth principle clarifies the process of documenting knowledge claims, research sources, paradata, methods, formats and standards. This is important in order to allow computer-based visualization methodology and findings 'to be understood and evaluated in relation to the contexts and purposes for which they are deployed' (ibid.). The last two principles indicate that, in order to avoid losing existing 3D visualizations of historical artefacts and places ('a growing part of human intellectual, social, economic and cultural heritage' [ibid.]), it is crucial to preserve their data (rather than the medium), enabling possible migration to future digital formats and ensuring long-term sustainability. Furthermore, the very creation of such visualizations should benefit 'the study, understanding, interpretation, preservation and management of cultural heritage' (ibid.) and provide access to historical information that is otherwise inaccessible.

The above principles are quite important not only for designing digital spaces and artefacts within them, but also for the navigation of knowledge. The concept of a *knowledge navigator* was first described by John Sculley, who was a CEO of Apple from 1983–93, in his 1987 autobiography, *Odyssey*. He referred to a device that is capable of accessing and searching large networked databases by using intelligent software agents. In October 2011, Apple introduced Siri – an application for iPhone OS (or iOS) – an intelligent personal assistant. This knowledge navigator is designed to help users find a place to eat, or choose a film to watch, or remind about pending appointments, and in the future Siri is also planned for in-car integration. The interaction with this application takes place via natural language user interface, which is still an area under investigation by computer linguistics professionals. This means that the more you use Siri the better it (or she?) understands you. Such an approach to knowledge navigation is predicted to be a key element for Web 4.0 technologies, allowing for 'intelligent interaction' with all sorts of electronic devices. Furthermore, the use of the agent technology (or, in other words, a graphical personification of computer software processes) dramatically enhances the intuitiveness of navigation. This relatively new technological reality involves a computational system that inhabits a complex, dynamic environment, where agents act as a communication interface and provide active, personalized assistance to users, who are involved in collaboration with a particular computer application. These software agents (also known as autonomous software programs) are able to perform simulations of human activities. They are able to learn the users' preferences and interests, make suggestions, function with minimal supervision and customize their assistance according to each participant. There are different 'habitats' which include, for example, computer games, VHEs and Second Life, and encourage different ways of communication for their users. The agents keep increasing the connectivity and interoperability with the real world, as well as improving their virtual 'liveability' and encouraging users to make best use of their creativity. In 2005, Cory Ondrejka (a Director of Mobile Engineering at Facebook and Advisory Board member of the Oxford Internet Institute) stated that existing media forms (such as books, films, games) are much more beneficial for us when they are social and will be much improved as they migrate into digital worlds, bringing disparate parts of knowledge together and existing in one accessible space. He also predicted that an increasing number of 'real-world' items (products and processes) will be planned and generated in collaborative spaces that can be leveraged both by corporations and *ad hoc* groups. As a matter of fact, such recent developments as HMV (the music and DVD chain, whose first store was opened in 1921 in Oxford Street in London) and Blockbuster (a provider of home movie and video game rental services) going into administration in January 2013 underlines the above forecast and illustrates that 'hard disk' media stores are struggling to compete with ever-expanding digital downloads and file sharing markets.

Indeed, the world around us has significantly turned to digital media for sharing information, history and cultural values. The next two chapters will look into how this influenced such fields of knowledge as theatre studies and cultural heritage research, elaborating on the above overview of existing and 'under-development' technologies, whose aim is to facilitate communication in digital spaces.

3

Art, history and culture in digital spaces

Abstract: This chapter investigates how existing cultural forms are redefined (and sometimes reinvented) through digital technologies. It looks into how the relationship between the artist, the viewer and the artefact has changed over recent years. The chapter examines an ongoing conflict between the 'virtual' and the 'material' in the museum environment, which has forced the definition shift of what exhibition spaces are and how the public perceives them. It analyses such factors as credibility and intellectual transparency when constructing a virtual heritage environment or when creating a 3D reconstruction of a historical artefact. It also discusses the importance of virtual presence for cultural heritage institutions and their approaches (and challenges) to addressing the issues of personalization, sharing and user feedback. The case study presented in this chapter attempts to address the problem of detachment between the viewer and the artefact by placing intangible historical events of the 1831 Nottingham Riots in context within immersive virtual spaces.

Key words: multimedia, 3D reconstructions, 'new institutionalism', virtual heritage, virtual heritage environment, cultural presence.

Digital technologies are in a constant process of redefining existing cultural forms, which often leads to the emergence of new ones. Multimedia (literally a blend of various types of media) embraces text, graphics, audio, animation and allows for a flexibility to convey information, knowledge and, furthermore, new qualities of communication. It could be argued that there are many possible readings of new media history, just as there are many possible paths through a network (Packer and Jordan, 2001). What is clear, however, is that digital technologies have irreversibly changed the way we produce, transfer and preserve our cultural values and have transformed the means we use to create artworks. Umberto Eco in his 1962 essay *Opera Aperta* (*The Open Work*) introduced the concept of *openness*, focusing on plurality in art. He attempted to explain the difference between traditional and modern art practices, describing the work of art as:

> a complete and closed form in its uniqueness as a balanced organic whole, while at the same time constituting an open product on account of its susceptibility to countless different interpretations which do not impinge on its unadulterable specificity. Hence, every reception of a work of art is both an interpretation and a performance of it, because in every reception the work takes on a fresh perspective for itself.
>
> (Eco, 1962: 4)

In other words, a modern artwork is a 'work in progress' with an 'indefinite reserve of meanings', which is even more so at present. Nowadays, the artefacts created exclusively for operating in virtual worlds, such as 3D reconstructions, digital installations or even virtual spaces *per se*, are regarded as artworks which can be experienced only digitally (Bolter and Grusin, 1999). Contemporary media artists create flexible structures and images with a variety of possible readings, placing the relationship between the artist, artefact and the viewer in a more behavioural context than in the past. The public, in its turn, has begun to actively participate in the act of creation on all levels of experience – conceptual, emotional and physical. Steven Willats, for example, emphasizes that art practice is a process-based experience with essential connections between 'the artwork', 'the audience' and 'the social context' (Willats, 2012). He argues that 'art as social process' extends well beyond the fact of the artwork itself, into the kind of society that will receive and recognize this art as legitimate practice (ibid.: 11D). Willats' approach to art-making focuses on breaking free from 'the culture of the collector', reinforcing a sense of identity amongst his diverse audiences and changing the status of the object 'from being a pedestal fetish to an agent of social interaction' (ibid.: 13B) Indeed, it could be observed from the current art practices that there is a need to rethink how cultural messages are delivered to viewers, shifting the focus towards their perception of historical narratives and artefacts, as opposite to the authoritarian point of view enforced by the media and art institutions. 'New institutionalism' – a term adopted from social sciences – emerged as 'a curatorial intention to create "an active space" that is "part community center, part laboratory and part academy"' (Möntmann, 2009: 155). Its goal is to encourage production of process-based artworks (opposite to the objects for passive consumption) aimed at promoting community participation and establishing dialogue with the art recipients. Computer-generated environments are often considered as a communication tool, as well as a logical extension of arts integration, thus supporting such an audience-centred attitude. Furthermore, some researchers might argue that digital spaces could act as an ideal place for applying the existing knowledge on human–computer interactivity. Contemporary creative practitioners experiment with new technologies, encouraging a consumer of art to interact closely with a machine, in order to create further interconnections between the two of them. The main goal of such interaction is to enable the user to participate in either fully-flexible or pre-programmed routines for the purpose of manipulating works of art. This (rather complex) exchange translated by the visual language of digital technology empowers artists to implement new forms of *production* – as opposed to *reproduction*. Thus, virtual worlds should not be defined in the context of their intended interpretations, but rather by the artefacts left behind. The argument here is that digital technology is not only a means for reproducing existing art styles and objects for the purpose of storing, studying or simply distributing them for mass-production, but also a platform for art creation. Despite all technological advances, it still cannot be predicted to what extent their further evolution will influence artistic vision. The artist's apprehension of technology is still very much an issue and, even these days, there is still only a small (but growing) number of creative practitioners who employ, for example, VR as a tool for making art. It could be observed that many such experiments are an exclusive art form that is locked in institutions and research centres, to be consumed by the academic elite but not that much by the general public. Undoubtedly, attempts to break with this tradition have been made over recent years and will be discussed in Part 4 of this book.

Different forms of art are unique in their definitions and use specific technologies of representation. More often than not, however, it takes a while for them to be accepted as an *art form*. Some time ago it happened to cinematography and, in its early years, also to VR, which, for some time, was considered as 'some sort of awful mechanized version of the true art' (Zellner 1999: 22). Although its significance for the art world has not been fully assessed as yet, VR provides numerous opportunities for artists to be creative, communicative and share their experiences. In

2011, Preston and Rogers introduced the notion of a *crisis of digitalization*. Their research focuses on one of the first areas to experience the influence of digital technological innovations – the sphere of music. They argued that artists can now 'produce, market and distribute recordings independently'; however, they still need the industry's traditional 'middleman' for selling their records in the 'mainstream' (Preston and Rogers, 2011: 16). A report by Ernst & Young, 'Monetizing digital media', published in 2010, expands on the above point, stating that technology has fundamentally changed how and where consumers access content, fragmenting audiences and revenue streams, and that media and enterprise companies have to learn how to defragment these relationships. The report further suggests that digital media content bundles will no longer be products, but will be value-added services, or media as a service (MaaS) – an ongoing relationship with the user. The same is happening to the software market, where the software as a service concept (or SaaS) has been implemented already. This development is beneficial for creators of virtual environments and ensures the continuity of graphic standards.

Over the last decade, digital graphics have become immensely popular and lucrative, forcing a new cultural definition of a computer. In the early 2000s, some art and media researchers were convinced that the work of art as a 'discrete object' was disappearing because of the inability of computer technology to record or reproduce the sensual presence of materialism in art, and that 'games and arbitrary interaction do not qualify the computer as a medium for memories and recollections' (Grau, 2003: 207). Nowadays, however, we witness the digital transformation of all major library and museum collections into interactive digital resources and displays, accessible to the wider public and mediated by a computer. In addition, technologies of computation are crucial in preserving our material culture, which is at the edge of vanishing or has already disappeared from the face of the planet, leaving behind scattered traces of its existence and, furthermore, making it accessible to contemporary media-savvy audiences (younger generations in particular). Sorin Hermon and Loukas Kalisperis (researchers from The Cyprus Institute) define cultural heritage as 'the legacy of physical artefacts and intangible attributes of a society, inherited from past generations and bestowed for future ones' (Hermon and Kalisperis, 2011: 59). According to the 2005 UNESCO handbook for teachers, a vast majority of developed countries have created free electronic archives, in an attempt to digitize their cultural heritage. Virtual presence is now an important agenda for all cultural heritage institutions, which poses a number of challenges not only to curators but also to designers of VHEs. A number of cross-EU projects (for example, MINERVA EC and MICHAEL) have taken place in an attempt to create a thematic network giving access to digitally preserved cultural artefacts and places. One of the most recent studies – the Virtual Museum Transnational Network, which began in 2011 and will last for four years – aims to provide the heritage sector with new tools and support (similar to SaaS) to develop museums in virtual spaces. Furthermore, such research clusters as the Museums Computer Group were established in order to set up discussion forums for museum, gallery, archive and higher education professionals who are engaged (or considered to work more closely) with new technologies. There are also studies that have been investigating the compatibility and incompatibility between museums and computation technology and examining the potential of interactive multimedia embedded in the delivery mode of cultural heritage exhibitions (Cameron and Kenderdine, 2007; Parry, 2007). For example, Andrea Witcomb argues that the majority of existing discussions in the field are based on a conflict between the notion of 'virtual' and 'material', as well as on an assumption that digital objects and environments cause 'a radical process of democratization' of current exhibition spaces (Cameron and Kenderdine, 2007: 35–48, in Kuksa and Tuck, 2011). Indeed, technologies of computation play an important role in shifting definitions of a museum space and one might even argue that new media have already achieved the status of 'materiality' (Witcomb, 2007). Besides, current debates in the field of museology suggest that there is a need to undertake 'reflexive re-assessment of the disciplinary orientation as well as the apparatus and practices of museum studies', with a major goal of producing innovative ways to rethink and to re-evaluate multi-level relationships between our society and culture (Whitehead, 2007; Message, 2009: 126). Nowadays, such museological practices as collecting, assembling and exhibiting heritage are not necessarily concerned with purely material inscription and embodiment of social knowledge nor limited to the museum environment. They extend beyond its physical borders into digital spaces, inevitably changing public perception of an exhibition display (Macdonald, 2006; Parry, 2007; Pujol and Champion, 2012). In 2012, Laia Pujol and Erik Champion suggested that virtual heritage (VH) should have six major aims. The first two are concerned with ensuring a careful capture and accurate (as well as engaging) presentation of the artefacts and processes of scientific, social and spiritual value. The next three aims stipulate that any VH project should be distributed in the most sensitive and durable manner to a long-term and the widest possible audience, providing them with a highly effective learning environment and with the possibility of contributing to its construction. The final aim states that the key to the success of any VH study is the continuous evaluation of not only the project and its outcomes but also of VH as a field of knowledge (ibid.: 86). These aims are very similar to London Charter's principles and guidelines for computer-based visualization of cultural heritage discussed in the previous chapter. These initiatives are very important for the development of the field and will hopefully address the issue of consistency (data storage, accessibility and sustainability) in VH projects and studies.

The construction of a VH environment comprises a number of the technical challenges mentioned above. What is even more important is the awareness of the VHE viewer of the intention of its producer. It is crucial to establish at the early stages of a VH project what approach to accessing information should be used – content- or user-oriented. The difference between the two is that the former allows the viewer to choose what to observe, but the latter, in addition to this, also tailors the experience to one's educational background and previous knowledge about the subject, which to date is still difficult to achieve in a museum environment (Hermon and Kalisperis, 2011). In comparison to social media platforms, VH has been slow to embrace multimodal forms of user interaction and their preferred ways of learning. Furthermore, such issues as personalization, sharing and feedback are still to be addressed in VH spaces. Despite this, as Erik Champion emphasizes in 'Otherness of place: game-based interaction and learning in virtual heritage projects': '[V]irtual heritage, for all its difficulties, can augment and afford experiential understanding via interaction in a way not always directly accessible through present-day cultural sites. Place can actually get in the way of cultural understanding for both the public and for archaeologists. What survives may not always be accurate, authentic, or revealing' (Champion, 2008: 210–11). Indeed, 3D visualization enables researchers to undertake more complex studies of the structure of a building or a monument than more conventional surveying techniques would allow. This approach, however, should involve careful management of the newly acquired content and could quite likely require new, more sophisticated software and hardware devices (Pavlidis et al., 2007; Andres et al., 2012). There are some concerns among researchers and professionals about the lack of sufficient documentation supporting the construction of 3D models, as well as some reservations that such models could misrepresent the existing 2D or (in particular) archaeological information, putting more emphasis on the artistic rather than the intellectual aspect (Hermon, 2008). If a variety of sources are considered, it is often the case that some of the data points are missing. This requires different levels of assumption and interpretation of available information. The important consideration to be made here is about adopting an open and intellectually transparent approach to all stages of 3D visualization. Some 3D developers argue that '[A]s long as the modeller is honest with the data used and the conclusions drawn, there can be no criticism of the process' and also suggest using colour coding where appropriate to illustrate the levels of certainty in 3D models to ensure their credibility (Jones, 2008). Despite some existing disagreement about the reliability of 3D visualization as a research method, numerous projects and studies of cultural heritage have established its benefits for the field. For example, digital reconstructions have been shown at such key exhibitions as *China Design Now* in the Victoria and Albert Museum (2008) and *Mummy: The Inside Story* in the British Museum (2005). Such displays not only emphasize the material inscription and objects, but also create a feeling of *cultural presence*. This concept was introduced by Erik Champion in 2005. It links together virtual reality and cultural heritage, combining 'the notion of "being there" with the communicational, social and contextual goals of heritage through the addition of symbolism, explicit expression of self-identity, and learning' (Pujol and Champion, 2012: 88). Champion also emphasizes the usefulness of virtual spaces from a constructivist perspective, which will be further explored in Part 3 of this book.

Thus, the construction of a virtual environment, 3D artefact or historical site is not purely a technical challenge. Such factors as credibility and intellectual transparency (if dealing with historical objects or archaeological sites) or audience engagement and feedback (if creating a piece of digital art or theatre) should be borne in mind. Nowadays, 3D records are becoming more popular and more widely accepted, stimulating new ways of interaction, communication and knowledge sharing. And although there is still a long way to go before digital artefacts or reconstructions are accepted as cultural attributes, the authors are in agreement with the following statement by Sorin Hermon and Loukas Kalisperis that 'we should regard visual communication in general and VR in particular, not as an "objective truth", parting from the Platonian perspective that "seeing is believing", but as only one truth amongst possible others' (2011: 621). Sometimes, however, this is the only truth available to the public.

Case 3.1 Exploring the Nottingham Reform Bill Riots through augmented reality (with Deborah Tuck)[1]

One of the goals of contemporary museums and cultural heritage sites is to address the issue of detachment between the viewer and the artefact in an attempt to present the audience with a variety of historical viewpoints. Such communication techniques as narrative are often used to transfer information about past events and, when placed in real-time virtual settings, provide an interactive and engaging way for the audience to experience history. These digitally-enabled stories transform conventional displays, placing intangible historical events in context within immersive virtual spaces. This study employed the interactive 'story world' format, in order to break away from the architectural walk-through type of traditional guided tourist trail in the City of Nottingham, emphasizing the recent change in preserving social history and cultural artefacts.

Nottingham's rich cultural heritage attracts approximately 300,000 overseas visitors every year. The city's key historical landmarks include its castle, the Galleries of Justice and Green's Mill. These important cultural sites constitute part of the Nottingham Tourist Trail, but geographically they are situated far apart from each other, which affects their accessibility to the general public. The above landmarks were of interest to the project team because of the significant role they played during the 1831 Reform Bill Riots. The aim of the study was to connect these historical buildings by scrupulously reconstructing them in 3D, placing them in a real-time immersive virtual environment, and linking them through a coherent multi-character narrative. To date, two of the participating sites are fully digitally visualized – Green's Mill and the Galleries of Justice. The latter is currently presented at the site itself in the form of a real-time narrated interactive tour of the lower parts of the building, which are difficult to access (particularly for visitors with limited mobility). The former is of more relevance to this volume, in terms of using digital spaces as 'small story worlds' (as opposite to a linear narrative) that are connected to each other through the history of the riots (Kuksa and Tuck, 2011). The 3D visualization of Green's Mill was firmly based on existing historical records, such as land surveys, ground plans and images from the photo archives (Figure 3.1).

Figure 3.1 **Designing the Green's Mill virtual heritage environment**

Source: from Tuck et al., 2009

Some of the original artefacts related to the storyline and hosted by a number of local collectors (public and private) were also digitized and placed in their 'natural' historical environment. In addition, a number of everyday objects had to be recreated artistically (because they no longer exist in reality) in order to make the space look in accordance with the relevant period. These visualizations, however, were also grounded in extensive archival research of newspapers, letters, diaries, drawings and paintings from 1790–1845. For example, one of the video narratives used in the VHE was based on the original oil painting by Henry Dawson, *Nottingham Castle on Fire, 10 October 1831*.

The Green's Mill VHE was generated with the help of the Quest3D real-time development engine and consisted of four core components (and see Figure 3.2):

- User navigation control system that interfaces with the user interactions with the mouse and keyboard and translates these actions to the participant's view and position in the virtual space.
- Event controller that determines the order in which events should be triggered based on the participant's location within the space, as well as their viewpoint.
- 3D scene rendering components that render elements from the 3D geometry database according to the current field of view of the participant.
- Post-processing component that re-colourizes and adds a soft-focusing filter to the virtual environment. This technique was employed to give the participant's perspective of the world

a more cinematic quality (as opposed to the typically sharp visuals within modern computer games), ultimately creating an atmosphere that further supports the idea of the 'story world' rather than 'reconstruction' (Tuck et al., 2009).

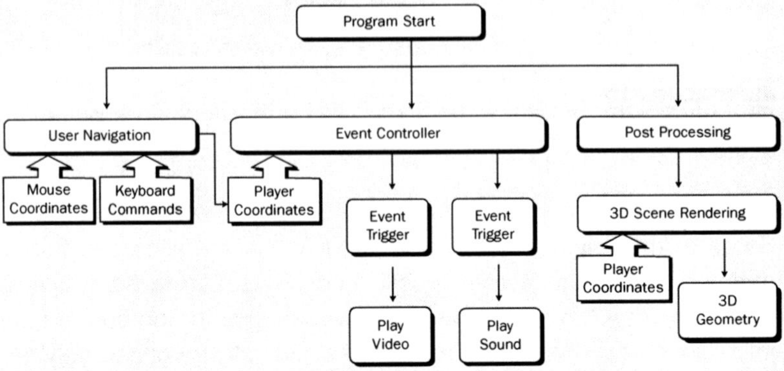

Figure 3.2 **Simplified structure of Green's Mill's virtual heritage environment**

Source: from Tuck et al., 2009

The Green's Mill VHE redeployed the following techniques widely used in the film industry, theatre and gaming. For example, the participant is given an opportunity to choose a 'walking' route to explore the environment, in order to select the sequence in which audio and video narratives are activated. The system uses several proximity triggers, which are instigated by the movement of the user and prompt the storytelling. These are also designed to fade and stop the narration should the user wander off, so they would have to walk back to hear the end of the story. To increase the likelihood of encountering the narratives, the pathways are designed to direct participants to the narration points with the help of such navigation aids as hedges, walls and paths, which are used to 'steer' them through the story trail. Users are only allowed to enter or exit the trail at specific locations. For example, after visiting the Mill and listening to several historical narratives, the participant can leave the yard through the only available side gate. Once through they cannot re-enter and are guided to the final narrative point by the 'ghosts' floating towards the poster tree, as well as by the sound of a courtroom. This scene encompasses an audio-visual, animated story about the trial of three rioters and a virtual portal to the Galleries of Justice, where this historical hearing took place (Figure 3.3). These are triggered by the proximity of the participant to the poster, and at the end of the narration the environment changes from one VHE (Green's Mill) to another (the Galleries of Justice). To understand the change in the settings and to avoid confusion, the participant is required to listen to the whole narrative without wandering off.

Figure 3.3 **The participant is guided to the focal point of transformation from one virtual heritage environment to another**

Source: from Tuck et al., 2009

To achieve this, the ability of the user to move about freely was restricted at this particular point. They could still 'walk' around a small 'collision' perimeter, which allows them to enter but not exit while the animated narrative is played. This method is widely used in gaming and also in film, in order to minimize the awareness of the viewer of the change from one shot to another, ensuring a smooth transition between the two. As can be seen from Figure 3.3, the tree poster is a focal point of this scene, designed to hold the focus of the participant's attention during the change from one VHE to another.

There is a strong progression of events integrated within the Green's Mill virtual environment, which aims at preventing the experience becoming a 'never-ending story'. The narratives are sequenced to be triggered one after another, meaning that the last narrative cannot be activated until the participant has heard the one before, which provides some background information to it (Figure 3.4). For example, upon entering the VHE the user is greeted by the 'voice' of George Green (famous mathematician and the owner of the Mill), and welcomed to explore the environment. The participant is also given some information about the site and then directed to the next story point.

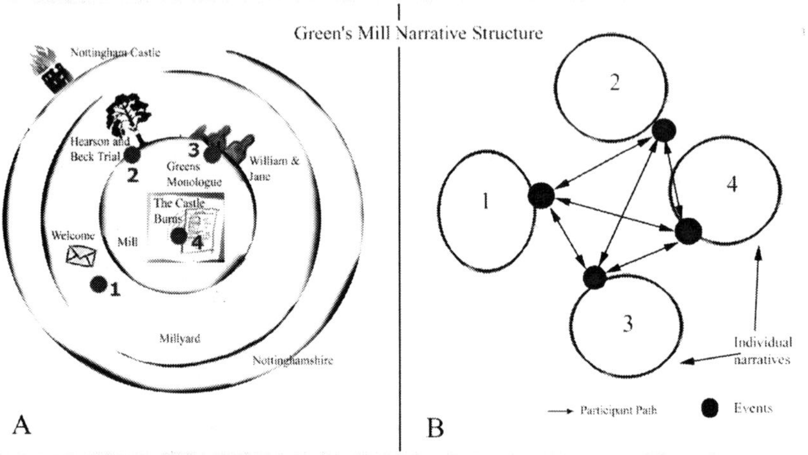

Figure 3.4 **Narrative structure (A) demonstrates the paths of participants exploring the virtual heritage anvironment and the 'story worlds' they encounter; (B) illustrates the non-linear narrative journeys the participant can take**

Source: from Kuksa and Tuck, 2011

Sound plays an important role in the Green's Mill VHE. It exists not only within the story spaces (when actual animated or video narratives are played) but also outside them (when users are simply wandering around). The atmospheric and environmental sound is applied to support the participant's sense of location via several 3D positional audio points integrated throughout the virtual site. This sound can be directed to the left or right speaker depending on the geographical orientation of the user in relation to the narration point. Furthermore, the volume level of every individual audio point could be raised (or lowered) depending on the participant's distance from it. Evidently, the Mill itself acts as a large landmark, which helps when navigating within the environment.

Sound, however, is also important in giving the user a more profound sense of place and direction.

All narratives used in the Green's Mill VHE were based on archival research and were created in consultation with Nottingham history and archaeology experts and participating heritage sites. To support the feeling of a 'living' environment and to bring more 'natural' experience to the user, it was decided to use embedded video narratives, instead of animated characters (or agents). The stories were narrated by professional actors and presented as semi-transparent images or shadows of the historical characters – a technique often used on the stage. The animation was employed, however, to create a fast dramatic scene in which to immerse the participant when the narrative is set around historical artefacts, such as the poster and the *Nottingham Herald* newspaper (digital copies of the original documents) – similar to the 'flash back' technique used in film. For example, when inside the Mill, the user sees a newspaper on the table with the front page containing a lithograph of Nottingham Castle on fire, published in October 1831. On their approach, the story of the event unfolds as a 3D animated model of the castle in flames, accompanied by the voice of the town crier. The whole environment darkens as the narrative progresses and the room fills with smoke and flickering fire effects, all of which disappear when the narration ends. This multi-narrative approach to storytelling allows the participant to feel more engaged with the historical content and empathize with the characters and their stories.

The Green's Mill VHE underwent two rounds of evaluation in 2009 by second-year undergraduate students in multimedia, audiovisual design and production at Nottingham Trent University. The results indicated a high level of immersion achieved by the participants and highlighted the ease of navigating within the VHE, although the length of some narratives was criticized. This issue has since been addressed by re-scripting and editing the longer narrations into more consumable sections. The respondents indicated that the 'story world' structure of the environment was beneficial to their learning about the history of Nottingham and had encouraged them to attend the real sites. Currently, the video of the VHE walk-through is part of the exhibition at Green's Mill, while the project team is working on integrating a multi-user option for navigating the VHE and input devices to allow participants to reflect on the experience by adding their own audio-visual and textual content.

Note

1. This case study was preliminary published in *International Journal of Arts and Technology* 4(4): 392–407, 2011 [DOI: *http://dx.doi.org/10.1504/IJART.2011.043447*] and in the Proceedings of the 2nd International Conference of Education, Research and Innovation (ICERI), 2009, pp. 1378–83.

4

Theatre in the virtual day and age

Abstract: This chapter investigates the effect digital technologies have on theatre, reconfiguring its aesthetics and challenging conventional audience–performance interaction. It analyses virtual reality as a space for theatre-making and attempts to answer the question of how the use of technology and artistic creativity can be balanced, in order to prevent the storyline from disappearing behind the 'new media decorations'. It is argued that technologies of computation offer a vast range of powerful tools for experiencing the art of theatre; however, it is emphasized that theatre-makers should identify the desired level of interactivity to maintain the feeling of the spectators' immersion and engagement with the performance. The case study presented here examines the 3D visualization of a scenographic artefact (Norman Bel Geddes' 1921 visualization of Dante's *The Divine Comedy*) as research methodology, bridging the gap between past and present theatre practices.

Key words: virtual theatre, enhanced theatre, digital scenery, virtual performance, cyber-audience, *fourth wall*, scenography, 3D visualization, Norman Bel Geddes.

Traditionally, live performing arts combine different media elements and support interaction and connection between the audience and the stage. In an historical sense, artists have always used impressive immersion tricks, such as physical surroundings with fake perspective, panoramic views or fresco images, to immerse the viewer in illusory reality. These attempts received further development with the advent of cinematography, computer technology and later VR. In 2002, Charlie Gere argued that multimedia proved to have a strong connection with, for example, the great cathedrals of Europe, the Dionysian rituals in Greek tragedy, and

Richard Wagner's concept of total artwork, in addition to a variety of other practices involving a combination of sounds, words and images (Gere, 2002). In 1849, Wagner defined drama as the ideal medium which united all separate branches of art including music, architecture, painting, poetry and dance, and embraced them in the 'collective art-work' and the 'synthesis of the arts' – the *Gesamtkunstwerk* (Wagner, 1849). He believed that this total artwork, this fusion of the arts, would attain 'new poetic heights' in theatre space. Randall Packer and Ken Jordan described Wagner's ideas as 'one of the first attempts in modern art to establish a practical theoretical system for the comprehensive integration of the arts through the "totalizing", synthesizing, effect of music drama – the unification of music, song, dance, poetry, visual arts, and stagecraft' (Packer and Jordan, 2001: xviii). The main feature of this system could also be described as immersion, experienced by the audience during theatrical performance, when spectators literally lose themselves in the veracity of the drama. Similar to Wagner's approach to the theatre with its scenery, lighting and acoustical design, Laszlo Moholy-Nagy's idea of the 'theatre of totality' foreshadowed the experience of virtual environments. It challenged the passivity of the relationship between the audience and stage performance by using innovative techniques for diluting the traditional *fourth wall* (in theatre terminology, the invisible frontier that divides the stage and the audience into two clearly perceptible parts) within the theatrical environment. His interpretation of Wagner's concept of 'total theatre' included the reduction of the importance of the written word and the presence of the actor. Instead, he developed the idea of the 'Mechanized Eccentric', which brought numerous technical devices into every aspect of the stage performance. Moholy-Nagy's machinery would travel across a multi-planed stage and would literally immerse the audience in the action. Everything and everybody – text, actors, stage design, lighting, music and visual composition – were equal in the theatrical space (in Packer and Jordan, 2001: 16–26).

In the late nineteenth and early twentieth centuries, the emergence of the modernist movement started the era of disillusionment with conventional expectations, reignited the interest in new technologies and promoted the freedom of expression and radical visions. The rejection of tradition and attempts to undermine conventional thinking were probably the most controversial aspects of modernism. Ironically, however, the rejection of tradition had become a tradition in its own right, which in the meantime has been interpreted by many researchers as the beginning of the postmodern era. However, there is much overlap between the two. Postmodernism, in its turn, brought forward many assumptions, one of which was that authenticity is no longer verifiable, and that something new can only be created through mixing existing art forms, styles, technology and media. Interestingly, at the beginning of the twentieth century the rapid development of recorded media was considered a threat to live theatrical performance. Since then, however, many sophisticated special effects based on current technological breakthroughs were introduced to the theatre, in order to enhance the element of 'spectacle' in various theatrical productions (particularly in musical theatre). Some of the technological innovations demanded specific modes of interaction and, as a result, the whole structure of performance arts began to change. Furthermore, in the late twentieth century new media technologies enabled theatre-makers to concentrate more on the emotional aspects of the theatrical experience. Christopher Baugh noted that '[T]he ability of the computerized theatre, as a newly endowed *Gesamtkunstwerk*, to operate with such intensity on this emotional level has generated a new, popular and strikingly populist form' – a contemporary musical theatre (Baugh, 2005: 210). In the early 2000s, a new type of theatre-maker and creative practitioner emerged. These new artists not only research such innovative techniques as interface design, virtual interaction and their freshly emerged forms, but also act as artists and scientists at the same time, in order to contribute to the development of the medium in key areas (in Grau, 2003: 3). They are inventive, imaginative and not restrained by technological limits; on the contrary, it is their responsibility to push the boundaries of technology itself. One might argue, however, that there is a strong polemical thrust to this statement. For some artists, the sophisticated communicative and creative possibilities provided by modern digital technologies still look impersonal, thus for many years a number of artists refrained from acknowledging that a computer is simply another tool to be used creatively if desired. The motives for not using digital technology for art creation are numerous, ranging from the inability of computers to generate 'true colour' to a general perception that their extensive use poses a threat to artistic creativity, in that machines are potentially taking over a thinking process. The logic here is partly flawed, because, for example, it is a fact that human beings can distinguish only a few million colours. Using twenty four binary digits (bits) – the smallest unit of information – on a machine means that about 16 million unique colours can be represented on a screen, which is enough to accurately visualize and perceive any colour image. On the other hand, however, a number of designers are contrary users of computer programs, in order to get unpredictable software responses, which, in fact, can be considered as allowing a computer to be responsible for the process of creation. It would seem that often the true reason for this scepticism about computers penetrating the art world is the lack of specialized knowledge and experience.

It could be argued that the art of theatre has many similarities to the phenomenon of VR. Some researchers, however, insist that despite the fact that theatrical performance 'has been extended, challenged and reconfigured by way of its position in the space of technology', at present it is obvious that 'there is nothing in cyberspace and the screened technologies of the virtual that has not been already performed on the stage' (Causey, 1999: 383). Although these courageous statements might appear to be overambitious, theatrical performance and the experience of virtual spaces indeed have a lot in common. Mark Reaney pointed out more than a decade ago that they are both 'time based, existing only during that time that the human participants are engaged with them. Both rely on the creation of a fictive universe designed to entertain, inform, and enlighten' (2000: 1). Any theatre environment is already a virtual space. It is a medium, which extends beyond the edge of traditional media such as film, television, radio, print and computer technologies, enabling very much an 'interfaceless' experience of the content. Furthermore, VR simulations possess such theatrical characteristics as passing from one virtual space to another, which is analogous with the change of scene, linking many spaces together to form a larger meta-space, suggesting varying degrees of visual and acoustic transparency, and explicitly or implicitly representing boundaries to the audience. All these features could be further intensified by various digital means, which offer an unlimited capacity for creating complex images and sounds that, if designed with care, are able to enrich the multi-textual nature of theatre. However, the question of whether these sophisticated simulations could offer something new still remains open for discussion. There are many theories about how new technologies of computation could potentially enhance existing theatrical techniques, some of which have been more or less successfully accomplished on stage. Ironically, however, there are not so many ideas about how digital media could influence the emergence of, for example, new forms of theatre. Usually, researchers are much more interested in speculating on the methods of delivering theatrical experience. In 1999, Dan Zellner stated that new digital technologies gave birth to two innovative types of theatrical space – the 'enhanced theatre' and the 'virtual theatre'. The enhanced theatre is situated in a physical environment with virtual scenery, inhabited by live and virtual actors. The virtual theatre, on the other hand, introduces a virtual performance that a single audience member can experience, while wearing a HMD. This type of theatrical space offers spectators a 3D performance that can be experienced in any location with computer input (Zellner, 1999: 27). This method of delivery has the potential to completely change the medium itself. On the other hand, however, it could potentially repeat the path of theatre on television, which attempted to bring a theatrical experience to mass audiences, sitting in front of their television screens at home. It can hardly be defined as a successful invention – theatre on television loses its liveliness, becomes absorbed by 'the logistics of television coverage' (Ridgman, 1998: 6), and becomes television. Thus, it is difficult to predict at present whether a new form of theatre or a new type of interactive computer game with live characters could emerge from such 'virtual reality–home theatre' concepts.

Nowadays, an increasing number of productions are getting 'immersed' in cyberspace, using the opportunity to reconfigure the meanings of art, theatre and technology – their aesthetics and ethics, societal beliefs, psychology – and, ultimately, by using various virtual reality devices – the artist–audience relationship. A good example here is the 2010 robotic opera, *Death and the Powers*, by Tod Machover, which was a collaboration between the American Repertory Theatre and MIT Media Lab. This unusual production introduced 12 fully functioning (and singing) robots, acting in parallel with human opera singers on-stage. The chorus of OperaBots (in addition to other props) was controlled by the unique software developed specifically for the occasion, which included a 3D visualization for creating and monitoring the animation of lighting and an absolute position tracking system for controlling robot movements and navigation. This production was recognized as a finalist for the Pulitzer Prize for Music in 2012. Despite this recent progress in staging performances, employing new media technologies, there are still numerous arguments about whether VR as a space for theatre-making is simply 'escapist' entertainment, where dramatic elements disappear behind technology, or whether it is an utterly self-sufficient and satisfying environment that contains all-important theatrical components. At present, there are still only a few theatre groups that produce small-scale VR productions, usually shown within an academic environment. These groups run on very tight budgets and cannot afford to pay for all the services required to produce a big professional show. As a result, they employ volunteers (usually university students), who join the production on an attachment basis. These arrangements could potentially jeopardize the overall quality of the staging, affecting even comparatively sophisticated technical productions; but, on the other hand, they could also promote a more flexible and daring approach to staging than, for example, a professional show. A good example here is the University of Kansas' experimental production of *The Magic Flute* (Reaney et al., 2004) which used a variety of real-time computer graphics projected on stage – quite an innovative technique for the early 2000s.

There is little doubt that interactivity enabled by digital technologies (as a new form of making and perceiving theatre) empowered set designers to create productions that are rich in information, imagery and storylines. As some researchers argue, these designs extend beyond the visual to the tactile, and rapidly change the time and the place in the course of a performance with little regard for physical limitations (see for example Cheok et al., 2002). The main idea here is to make the audience responsible for binding together the plot of the performance, which is sometimes difficult to achieve when conventional scenographic techniques are employed. Commonly, designers translate their artistic intentions into technical instructions; however, the employment of digital space as a design tool increases the flexibility of visual research and combines it with 3D modelling, 'intelligent' lighting and movement applications. Furthermore, it invites creative practitioners to play and experiment, facilitating unconventional ideas and ultimately the construction of unique theatrical sets. New virtual staging techniques can enhance or, as one might argue, replace traditional theatre design with flexible, computer-generated sets that (unlike video or animation) are not pre-recorded and can be manipulated during a real-time performance. Digital scenery is perfectly able to reflect the development of the plot, it is unique to every theatre piece, and it is portable and adaptable to almost any theatrical space. Theatre researchers and computer scientists conduct numerous experiments with live webcasting, in order to discover how the Internet could be used to share live theatre. For example, some interactive performances are connected via the web or satellite, and staged in real time to audiences at several physical locations. Simultaneously, other artists (also via the Internet) can be invited for input participation. This means that externally transmitted video images, sound-samples, voices and texts can be instantaneously integrated and layered onto the video projection and sound mix in the real space. Additionally, the real-time performance can also be recorded with digital cameras and projected into the virtual space. Furthermore, some of the research projects are concerned with creating virtual spaces (mainly in Second Life) that are inhabited by avatars or virtual characters controlled by participants from remote locations. These technology-oriented studies have their main focus on research and education and could potentially inform professional theatre practice. As seen from above, any interaction between the participant and live action, which is enabled by new technologies of computation, has two sides – real and virtual. The viewers can be present in the actual physical space and, simultaneously, in the virtual environment perceiving the same virtual or real-time happening or performance. The first kind of interaction could only occur if a theatrical event happens in real time and space. Here, some of the audience members are physically present in the auditorium, while others are virtually represented (for example, as holographic images) through telepresence devices. The virtual spectators have nearly the same opportunity to influence the flow of the performance, responding to the on-stage action and contributing to the creation of a special theatrical atmosphere. In the second case, the spectacle, as well as being performed live in virtual space using, for example, the Internet engine or motion capture technology, could potentially be pre-recorded. If this happens, however, VR theatre could become similar to theatre performances on television.

The perspective of being fully immersed in virtual space may fascinate many theatre researchers and modernizers; however, at the present stage of technological development a total transfer of users' senses from the real world into the virtual cannot be tested without the existing restrictions of wearable devices. This implies that body movements have to be recorded inside a computer, which, due to current limitations in computer processing capacities, significantly reduces the number of participants who can be transferred simultaneously into virtual performances in cyberspace. Furthermore, every theatre performance has unique moments of improvisation on stage and unpredictable reactions from the audience. If spectators are 'virtual' (or represented by the avatars) they might greatly affect the flow of the performance. According to reception theorists (for example, Hall, 1980 and Bennett, 1997), the recipient (a reader or a viewer) actively interprets (decodes) the meaning of an artwork, a text or a performance, encoded by the producer. These interpretations are based on such factors as their cultural background, beliefs and life experiences. Sometimes the recipients adopt different (even opposite) stances on the intended (by the creator) meaning. Cyber-audiences are not an exception. They are able to respond by using multimedia tools such as web cameras and microphones to broadcast their reaction. This process can quite possibly get out of control (especially if the performance is live) and may provoke a situation where the important narrative events will never be experienced. It could be argued that by reducing interactivity in multimedia systems, the author of a narrative obtains much more control over the users' experience of key events in virtual environments. If a theatrical event takes place in non-immersive cyberspace, the scenery appears as the interface that a contemporary audience could have on their computer screen. It also provides the feeling of distance, which can also be classified as the *fourth wall*, implying that, at least in this regard, the relationship between the virtual actors and the audience is guaranteed (Wunderer, 2002: 203). On the other hand, however, such constrained interactivity may reduce the feeling of the spectators' immersion and engagement with the performance.

The above discussion raises the question of how to balance the use of technologies for theatre in order to provide new insights into audience–performance interaction. Evidently, computer technologies offer a vast range of powerful tools for experiencing theatre space, as well as for creating it. However, they are not able to solve every single technical problem that could potentially arise. As a matter of fact, they could even cause a failure to perform, if the computerized system collapses. Contemporary musical theatre is a good example in this regard – there, almost all scenic elements are run by computers, and the success of the whole performance depends upon their smooth operation. Similar to most designs, if overused it may cause the storyline to disappear 'behind the decorations', ultimately leading to performances that lack artistic depth. Therefore, this question should be considered carefully by each individual theatre-maker.

Case 4.1 Scenography reborn in 3D

For more than a decade, one of the main goals of new media-oriented projects has been to explore new ways of experiencing art, performance, entertainment and culture in general within increasingly popular mixed-reality environments. Nowadays, learners are given an opportunity to control the way they consume new knowledge, through actively engaging with course resources, which, in turn, have become increasingly technology based. When teaching theatre history and scenography, new technologies can serve as an appropriate medium for a visually-enhanced communication of past theatrical events and artefacts. Virtual learning environments (VLEs) engage their users imaginatively, intellectually and interactively, giving them a wide range of choices with which to confront and manipulate historical information. 3D visualization of historical works of art, design and architecture has recently been established as a new research methodology. Scenographic artefacts are a crucial link in bridging the gap between past and present theatre practices, and their visualization in 3D is often possible and even necessary for scholarly analysis (Kuksa, 2007). The creation of the 'new' (3D model) and reconstruction of the 'old' (historical artefact) can be successfully combined and can greatly enhance each other. There is, however, a shortage of educational products in the field of scenographic history that employ innovative visualization techniques (such as virtual imaging or 3D simulations of theatrical artefacts) combined with hypertext and other rich media content. Thus, the research project 'in progress' discussed below aims to address the issue by developing a comprehensive, interactive, educational platform to support the study and research of modernist scenographic artefacts, through employing innovative technological means of knowledge reconstruction, presentation and delivery. It aspires to provide new insights into the role and importance of Norman Bel Geddes (1893 1958), a pioneer of American stage design whose creative outputs and contributions to the development of modernist scenography have remained largely overlooked. Methodologically, the project proposes to use cutting-edge computer technologies to reconstruct the designer's key stage concepts, which will not only enable innovative, original research on these artefacts, but also provide exciting, novel opportunities for theatre education and knowledge dissemination.

Norman Bel Geddes was involved as author and/or designer in more than 200 plays, theatrical performances and motion pictures. He was also a talented and successful industrial designer identified with the popular 1930s 'streamlining' style in the US. While scholars generally agree on the historical importance of Bel Geddes' industrial designs and widely criticize his architectural projects, his impact on theatre design is largely overlooked, or at least misjudged. Originally named Norman Melancton Geddes, he transformed his name using the prefix Bel, which he borrowed from his first wife, Belle Sneider. This rather eccentric pairing served Bel Geddes well during his professional career, which extended across one of the most interesting periods of artistic and theatre history in North America. Bel Geddes was a devoted follower of the early twentieth-century New Stagecraft movement, which gave birth to numerous visionary scenographic projects. In Europe, Adolphe Appia and Edward Gordon Craig laid the foundations of an entirely new type of stage setting and lighting design. The strong philosophical, conceptual and visual basis of their works had a profound impact on Norman Bel Geddes, and inspired his ambition to become one of the core modernist stage designers in the US. Bel Geddes' remarkable productivity and his ability to combine creative thinking with technical knowledge were reflected in his designs. His futuristic concepts and desire to make the world 'cleaner, safer, prettier, and better for all' (Roberts, 1979) by employing advances in science and industry can be defined as 'hope-giving' to the economically depressed America of that time. Together with other followers of the New Stagecraft movement, such as Lee Simonson and Robert Edmond Jones, Bel Geddes employed an expressionistic stylization, which emphasized psychology and emotional states throughout the play. However, the over-complexity of Bel Geddes' concepts, frequent underestimation of production costs, and his lack of flexibility in the modification or adaptation of his sets to a particular theatrical space, resulted in a number of unaccomplished projects. Nevertheless, his visionary set designs rivalled those of Adolphe Appia and Gordon Craig in shaping the evolution of twentieth-century scenography. Unfortunately, however, 'no scholar has judged Bel Geddes worth a monograph; and his name is barely remembered except by experts in American theatre history' (Innes, 2003).

The purpose of this study is to address a shortfall in educational provision in two areas. Specifically, there is a lack of awareness of the work of Norman Bel Geddes within modernist theatre and the scenography subject area and amongst the wider public. More generally, this work elaborates on the findings of previous research on 3D visualization of historical artefacts and takes them to a new level. The digital reconstruction of Bel Geddes' set concepts is envisioned ultimately as a source of knowledge, but also as a catalyst for creating new educational and design applications and customizing the teaching curriculum in the field of theatre studies. Theatre education has always balanced the demands of theory and practice. The history of scenography, however, is often delivered verbally with some visual aids, and often lacks an external, interactive and creative element of learning. Thus the aim of this study is to evoke new associations, meanings and values that can reshape the conventional construction of teaching and learning about set design and theatrical artefacts. While this project seeks to be comprehensive, it would be overambitious if it tried to be exhaustive or conclusive. Presented in a flexible digital format, it is open for further development. The process of exploring Norman Bel Geddes' collection will involve both ascribing metadata to the resources (based on recommendations outlined in the London Charter), and scanning and storing them within a digital repository. Through the building of the 3D models, it is anticipated that new insights into Bel Geddes' work will be realized, both from an aesthetic and a practical point of view. The merits and barriers of using this methodology (in particular the creative element of it) will also be assessed. This will help fellow academics to adopt this tool for their teaching and research, having an impact on the HE community as a whole. In an educational arena, the research approach and methodology this project proposes will be of value to academics studying best practices in learning and teaching, as well as to those experimenting with technology to achieve best possible knowledge transfer. This study will investigate the means through which archival resources and their 3D visualizations can be adopted in educational programmes (both in university degree courses and in museum-located activities), aiming to provide guidance on and exemplars of effective routes to incorporating these forms of materials into learning practices. In addition, the interactive activities, in which learners use their creative side (for example, illuminating the 3D set models and interacting with a variety of textures), will also be of interest to academics studying the impact of constructivist learning on students' engagement and achievement. In addition, this project provides opportunities to use visual technologies to improve public engagement with artefacts and their history in museums and heritage sites.

The research for this study was conducted in the Harry Ransom Centre, University of Texas at Austin, where the most comprehensive collection of Norman Bel Geddes' industrial and theatre designs resides. The main focus of archival research was on examining his theatre, correspondence and publicity files and duplicating relevant 2D materials (visual and textual). To date, 3D visualization of Bel Geddes' 1921 set concept for Dante's *The Divine Comedy* (arguably the most remarkable of his set designs) is fully realized and hosted by the Ransom Centre. It has also been successfully integrated into the teaching curriculum of several UK universities, proving the demand for this type of approach to the delivery of visual knowledge. Furthermore, it was part of the first (posthumous) major exhibition of Bel Geddes' key design concepts, *I Have Seen The Future: Norman Bel Geddes Designs America*, which took place in the Ransom Centre from September 2012–January 2013. And in autumn 2013, this unique exposition was on display in the Museum of the City of New York. Data for the rest of the visualizations was collected in November 2012 and is currently being analysed.

3D visualization of The Divine Comedy

Norman Bel Geddes' imaginary concept for Dante's masterpiece, conceived in 1921, aimed to mark the six-hundredth anniversary of the poet's death. The scale of this stage construction was extraordinary, with sophisticated machinery and numerous sound and lighting effects – which one might define as too advanced for the beginning of the twentieth century. The production was supposed to total 523 actors and was envisaged by Bel Geddes to take place in Madison Square Garden. It took him approximately two years to develop a fully functional wooden model (a twenty-fourth of the full size of the real set construction measuring

135 ft × 165 ft) which was lost during the last century. The stage model was incredibly detailed, in order for the set to be rapidly constructed in an actual theatre. Despite being carefully designed, this set concept was far too big a challenge for contemporary theatre practitioners and investors and remained unrealized for the rest of Bel Geddes' life, despite his constant attempts to stage it. Before 3D visualization technologies became available, the record of this masterpiece of modernist stage design included 60 black and white photographs (by Francis Bruguière) of the model equipped with plaster figures of the actors and accurate illumination, which was arranged according to the intended plot, a number of renderings, sketches, as well as blueprints and elevations. The precision of the above 2D resources was key for generating an accurate computer model. There are, however, some minor irregularities in the width of the front steps and the shape of the towers, which possibly occurred because the front elevation was projected from perspective drawings instead of architectural plans. This inconsistency would not have affected the overall structure of the stage nor, importantly, its functionality, and was clearly described (and visually illustrated) while creating the 3D visualization of the set (Figure 4.1). Students and researchers were/are encouraged, however, to question the reconstruction of *The Divine Comedy* set, using the contextualization of the model with primary source materials.

Figure 4.1 **The evolution of *The Divine Comedy* case study: from the archive to the classroom**

Source: Kuksa and Childs, 2010

The graphics for 3D model and lighting controls were rendered in Direct3D 9 Library, with the programming for navigation accomplished in Integrated Development Environment (IDE) Visual Studio 2005, using C# object-oriented language. The sources of lighting, which users can employ creatively for illuminating the 3D model from various viewpoints, were written (and stored) using a flexible text format Extensible Markup Language (XML).

In order to create visual effects based on Bruguière's photography while interacting with the digital set, the decision was taken to apply light colours and smooth texture to the model (Kuksa, 2008b). By experimenting with directional and spotlight sources, the viewer can create a unique dramatic atmosphere, corresponding with (for example) the original text by Dante. In 2008, *The Divine Comedy* 3D model was used as a teaching tool at the University of Warwick to introduce second-year theatre and performance undergraduates to new ways of studying historical artefacts and interpreting classical texts. During this practical session, students were given two of Dante's passages to analyse and were asked to create two digital sketches, visualizing their findings. Students used interactive white boards for recording and saving their ideas in real time and presenting the results (Kuksa and Childs, 2010). This exercise was successful in boosting students' motivation and creativity, proving that there is scope for bringing novel technology-based models of learning about 'lost' historical artefacts into the classroom.

This project is the first major study of Norman Bel Geddes and his contribution to the development of modernist theatre and the New Stagecraft movement in the US and Europe. Once the remainder of his set concepts are visualized in 3D, the resource will become a more widespread tool for education, not only within HE, but also within the museum and galleries sector.

Conclusion

Digital spaces offer a number of new opportunities to enhance (and change) the processes of art and theatre-making and history preservation. Numerous paradigm shifts and technological breakthroughs in software and hardware development enabled the users to interact with digital objects and navigate digital space in an arguably 'natural' way. At the beginning of the millennium, the majority of information technology scientists were convinced that the next generation of computers would be embodied (or personified) appliances. Indeed, the most recent developments in mobile digital technologies illustrate a clear shift towards numerous display and screen devices of different sizes, leading towards 'framed' observation of this day and age. However, there is a tendency within academic circles to advocate that this highly-technological but 'framed' approach to creating performance space is not desirable. Critics believe that because the viewers (of a digital artwork, or a performance, or a 3D heritage site) might not be able to abstract themselves from these numerous surrounding frames, the very nature of interaction (and communication) could be jeopardized. It is highly unlikely, however, that younger generations of technology users (digital natives who have been surrounded by various screen technologies from very early childhood) would even perceive a delivery medium between them and a virtual space as a frame. It remains quite arguable, however, whether computer technology can enhance 'real' creativity, as opposed to *technicality*, although one might argue that technicality could also be creative. Obviously, the technological capacity of computers is not unlimited and should be carefully balanced when used for the creation of an artwork. The question of when technology should be involved and when not must be answered by each individual artist. Additionally, there is a risk that creative practitioners no longer concentrate on art *per se*, but become absorbed by the fascination of technological innovations. Such an approach to creative practices, however, is becoming a thing of the past; with artists increasingly concerned about the intellectual and philosophical implications of their work. The use of new technologies in arts and humanities creates a lot of scope for desirable attempts to break with conventions, but it has to be done with care – otherwise it will be merely an end in itself. The most important aspect of creativity in technology-based creative practices is keeping the focus on art, not on technology.

Note

1. This case study was preliminary published in the Proceedings of the 3rd Digital Interactive Media in Entertainment and Arts Conference (DIMEA), 2008, pp. 62–8; in *Theatre Design and Technology* 44(4): 49–57; and in *Learning Media and Technology*, 2010, pp. 275–91.

Part 3
Experiencing virtual spaces

5

Two models to conceptualize space

Abstract: This chapter describes the ways in which digital and virtual spaces are experienced. It argues that the open exploration of spaces and the temporary and random encounters within them give rise to the sense of virtual worlds as being an inhabited place. The chapter discusses the emotional agency with which we imbue spaces and introduces the concept that virtual places require the engagement of belief. This concept is accompanied by a discussion of Activity Theory and its use as a framework to describe the elements and context for experience. The omissions of Activity Theory in its role in understanding the experience of virtual worlds are identified as the situated experience of being in the space, and as the aspects of identity that are employed within that space. These are found in the concepts informing the Communities of Practice model and so a mash-up of these two frameworks is suggested, named extended Activity Theory.

Key words: presence, *Dasein*, Activity Theory, Communities of Practice, navigation, wayfinding, rhizomatic space, engagement of belief, extended Activity Theory.

Living in virtual spaces

In the book *Virtual Literacies: Interactive Spaces for Children and Young People* (Merchant et al., 2013) a variety of practitioners discuss their experiences of children's education and literacy in a range of online environments. One of the chapters, entitled 'Seeking planning permission to build a Gothic cathedral on a virtual island', recounts and analyses a series of forum postings between teenagers and adults about whether it was appropriate for one of the students to build a Gothic cathedral in the shared space of the virtual world used by the project (Gillen et al., 2013). The authors of this chapter were all staff members working on the Schome Initiative[1] – an online project hosted by the Open University in the UK. The intention of this venture was to provide an educational system based on online interactions, which was neither school nor home, hence the name. As part of this initiative, Schome Park Island was created on the Teen Second Life grid, where young people could interact with their peers and adult facilitators, as well as build structures within the space. The debates described in the chapter included the aesthetics of Gothic architecture, and the rights of religious freedom and its appropriateness within the public domain, from the perspectives of respecting religious observance and of not unduly exposing people to its influence. The young participants' involvement in the discussion was very personal and emotional, without being confrontational. It was clear, however, that the presence of the 3D cathedral on the island (as opposed to uploaded imagery) affected young contributors to a great extent. In part, this happened because the building of a cathedral involved an act of creation, but also because the technology itself is exceptional in the emotional agency that it enables or provokes, meaning that the forms of interaction are imbued with an emotional element. For their users, virtual worlds are not simply an image on a 1366 × 768 pixels monitor (to take the example of the laptop on which this chapter is being written), they are lived environments, which are not simply seen, they are *inhabited*.

The experience of spatiality

The clarification of the distinction between observing a space and being in it is something that philosophers such as Spinoza, Coleridge and later Heidegger have long struggled with (Dreyfus, 1991: 15–16; Blake et al., 2007: 291). Heidegger employed the term *Dasein*, which translates from German as literally 'being there'. This could be described as a foreshadowing of the current definition of psychological immersion and interpreted to mean that our existence is grounded in the physical location of where we are. For Heidegger, as Hubert Dreyfus argues 'we are not merely present in a space; our existence is constructed from our relationship to that space' (Dreyfus, 1991: 141–4). The distinction was further articulated at a later date by a French phenomenological philosopher, Maurice Merleau-Ponty, who described a body as situated (as opposed to merely located) in a space, implying that it has a relationship to the objects and tasks surrounding it (Smith, 2007: 16). According to Dreyfus, *Dasein* is more fundamental than a mental state, because it is not 'a conscious subject', which is a reference to Heidegger's statement that '[T]he intentionality of "consciousness" is grounded in the ecstatical temporality of *Dasein*' (Dreyfus, 1991: 13–14).

Heidegger's description of 'ecstatical temporality' captures the different quality of experience of moving through the space of a virtual world, as opposed to navigating a website, or even altering the camera position in a 3D image. Virtual worlds are persistent in the sense that the elements of them remain while the user is logged off, but at the same time they are still very fluid places. Buildings can be taken down and replaced overnight, objects can be removed or added with a simple drag and drop, and even the terrain itself can be altered. In addition, the presence of avatars and their motions are never the same twice. Each visit to a virtual world is unique; and a visitor knows that whatever occurs is ephemeral. Although the visit can be recorded from a single viewpoint using screen capture software, the potential for spontaneity and for serendipity is lived and then gone. This gives Heidegger's 'ecstatical temporality' a new and technological form.

The movement as one takes steps through a digital environment also resonates with the experience of moving through the physical world. This spatial navigation relies not just on the graphics card of the user's laptop, but also on the processing power of the user's hippocampus, which is part of the limbic system of the brain (Patel and Vij, 2010: 101) and the most basic part of human cognition and memory. There are three aspects of spatial navigation: a cognitive component known as wayfinding (already mentioned in previous chapters), and two motor components consisting of locomotion and manoeuvring (Bowman, 2002: 281; Darken and Peterson, 2002: 494), discussed below. An essential part of wayfinding is the development and application of a cognitive (or mental) map (ibid.). It is this mental image of the space in which we are situated that is stored in and retrieved from the hippocampus. Our spatial cognition goes through three steps in the building up of a picture of space, enabling it to be navigated. The first of these steps is familiarizing oneself with the key locations in the environment. Although focusing on these milestones enables some recognition and orientation, the knowledge of the space at this stage consists of a disconnected set of landmarks, which become linked together to form a series of routes in the second stage. In the third stage (and after more exposure), a more flexible, map-like representation of the space is built up. This is sometimes referred to as a survey representation or as configurational knowledge (Patel and Vij, 2010: 102). Identifying one's relationship with landmarks, and plotting routes between them, is more difficult in a virtual environment because the view of it is usually restricted to a flat 17", 15" or 11" screen, rather than surrounding the user. For this reason, many virtual world interfaces include close-range and long-range maps to help with wayfinding. This helps the user to become experienced at blending information between the immediate viewpoint of the camera and the larger-scale bird's-eye view of the 'mini-map' and the world map.

Locomotion techniques in virtual worlds can be divided into naturalistic (walking, vehicular) and magical (flying, telekinesis, teleportation) (Bowman, 2002: 283). Manoeuvring is the smaller set of movements such as turning around or taking incremental forward- or side-steps, which result in a change in orientation or perspective but not in altering location (Darken and Peterson, 2002: 494). However, within the context of a virtual world, which is both a mixture of real (in the sense of possessing normal Euclidean dimensions and recognizable artefacts) and also fantastical (in that the laws of physics can be turned on and off on demand), the distinction between magical and naturalistic is reduced or non-existent. The different locomotion techniques are all integrated seamlessly through the keyboard controls, so, for example, in some virtual world technologies a quick tap on a Page Up button causes one's avatar to leap; holding down the same button for an extended time transforms this into flight. The way in which the avatar is animated also smoothly moves the action from one of naturalistic movement to one of magical, normalizing what might also be a jarring experience. Among the highly positive responses given by users of virtual worlds are the expressions of exhilaration at the new forms of motion that can be experienced. These forms are both familiar and unfamiliar and it is often the magical ones that make the strongest first impressions. Manoeuvring is often the most difficult for new users. Minor alterations to position and orientation require more precise control than the other forms of navigation, and often combining locomotion movements with small changes in orientation is a frustrating experience. It is an example of how inverted the common-sense nature of virtual worlds can sometimes be that walking up stairs is a more difficult task to master than flying.

The spatiality of virtual worlds enables the user to *encounter* objects and other beings, not just see them, which aids the development of a cognitive map. Teleportation, however, could have the effect of collapsing spatiality, when one disappears from one place and reappears somewhere else. This means that the sense of a unified and concrete space is momentarily removed, but is soon re-established when the user is back to the normal 3D arena of interaction. The serendipitous nature of meeting others, interacting intentionally (and unintentionally) with objects and structures, and the spontaneous occurrence of events encountered within such environments, all contribute to Heidegger's 'ecstatical temporality'.

As part of the Theatron[3] Project,[2] a group of performance studies students were interviewed about their experiences of exploring the use of Second Life for performance. The project ran from 2007 to 2012 and was directed by Richard Beacham at the King's Visualization Lab in the Department of Digital Humanities at King's College London. A number of 3D models of historical theatres were either imported from the previous versions of the project or developed specifically for Second Life and placed on an island there. All models were accompanied by explanatory data (called paradata) and interactive tools to support the use of these theatre spaces as sites for research, education and performance. One of the groups of participating students worked with the Commedia dell'Arte stages over several months, at the end of which they were interviewed about their experiences. Their responses are indicative of this sense of exhilaration with the aforementioned forms of movement and the types of interaction these arenas are open to. As one student stated, 'It's something new and it's different. There are no boundaries; you can just fly off somewhere. One second you're in the Globe and then you're somewhere else.'

The openness of these spaces, the endless possibilities that can emerge and the freedom to travel (almost) anywhere are responsible for eliciting the ecstatical temporality of that moment. This ever-present exhilaration of the experience of *now* gives rise to the feeling of being situated within the world, not simply located within it.

Emotional agency in virtual spaces

One of the Theatron[3] students spoke about their contrasting experiences of Orientation Island and the Holocaust Museum in Second Life. Orientation Island is the space designed by Linden Lab to induct new users. It consists of a series of tasks which explain the locomotion techniques, how to interact with objects, how to chat with other users and how to alter the appearance of one's avatar. To reach each stage in the induction, the user has to move through a predetermined path. The stages are programmatic, and sometimes difficult to master, which can form an initial and detrimental impression of the experience; the student described this as 'not really the thing because it was like a computer game'. Thus, this stage is sometimes referred to (ironically) as

'Disorientation Island'. The Holocaust Museum recreates Kristallnacht, and the student had found this latter experience deeply moving. It had conveyed for the first time the emotional agency that is possible within the virtual world, whereas the simple game-like scenario at the start had not. Once awakened to the sense of the world as somewhere they could inhabit (as opposed to something which they could only point and click on), the students went on to explore further, describing this as a process of '[G]oing round seeing what sort of world they are in'.

The above comparison of the 'game-like' Orientation Island and the freedom of the rest of the environment recalls Murray's division of spaces into maze-like and rhizomatic (Murray, 1997: 130). The maze has only one correct path through it, whereas the rhizome spreads out in many directions and repeating a journey through this space is rarely the same twice (ibid.: 135). The rhizome metaphor draws attention to the idea of knowledge being formed in a series of nodes, developing incrementally and independently, and without a recognizable centre or boundaries. The two metaphors come together in the design of many learning activities in virtual words, in which participants incrementally build up an understanding of the subject matter while walking around the environment. These designs often permit students to either travel on a designated route or choose to explore the world rhizomatically. Some evidence indicates that the latter enables students to feel greater immersion and, as a result, their learning experience is more effective (Nadolny and Childs, in preparation).

Once this emotional connection with the space is experienced, the theatres recreated in the virtual world are not just objects, they are spaces, with atmosphere, but this atmosphere is not simply generated by the environment. As one of the students in the Theatron[3] Project stated:

> It's not just the idea round the theatres, we actually have to perform in different spaces to get the atmosphere. Because we've got the atmosphere, because you can play around with the characters and make the audience be back in that century, it encourages as an audience member to actually think 'Wow, we've actually been transformed.'

It is true that the spatiality facilitates this feeling, but it is the intentionality of action and performance by the student that evokes the sense of inhabitation. It is only when the participant engages these conscious faculties that they can transform what is otherwise only a peripheral and disconnected view of events on a screen to a fully immersed journey through a space of which they feel part. Through inhabiting the space the emotional impact is not only inculcated in the performer, it encourages other participants to be drawn into this sense of belonging. And through finding the emotion in spatiality they are no longer simply users – they are residents.

The engagement of belief

The introduction to this book stated that the crux of the idea of VR is that the quality of the user involvement depends on their willing suspension of disbelief. What emerges from the students' accounts is that this suspension of disbelief is not necessarily easy to acquire and it varies from one person to another. Carrie Heeter states that only one in four participants will easily suspend their disbelief in a VR, one in four will always have difficulty in the process, and the remainder will fall somewhere between these two points. She hypothesizes that the reason for this is that some people are 'so strongly situated in the real worlds and their real body that they have a difficult time becoming involved in the virtual world' (Heeter, 1995: 200). This does appear to be confirmed by some students participating in the Theatron[3] Project, particularly by those who recounted a strong preference for physical games and an aversion to computer games. Heeter actually uses the phrase 'engage belief' rather than 'suspend disbelief', underlining the active and volitional nature of this leap of faith, rather than the act being a negation of an absence. She refers to the distinction between these two tendencies as the 'Peter Pan Principle'. Max and Sarah North and Joseph Coble further observe that 'the sense of presence in virtual and physical environments is constant and subjects have to give up the sense of presence in one environment (e.g., physical environment) to achieve a stronger sense of presence in the other one (e.g., virtual world)' (North et al., 2002: 1075). The processes of connecting with the virtual space and disconnecting from the physical one can be classified as 'arrival' and 'departure' (Sadowski and Stanney, 2002: 792). In general, however, it is quite possible for participants to be split between worlds, dividing their overall sense of psychological immersion. For the majority of students, their 'departure' from the physical world and 'arrival' in the virtual world was of sufficient depth and duration that they became emotionally connected with their experiences there. For one student, who did not detach from the real world, the experience was simply one of 'staring at the screen for ages'; psychological immersion had not taken place.

Not all online environments require users to be Peter Pan in order to get the most out of them. In fact, most do not. Websites that convey information, or social networking sites that facilitate interaction through the sharing of text and photos, do not necessitate the engagement of belief in the space to get the full experience. Without spatiality, they neither locate nor situate the user within the environment. One of the Theatron[3] students described the difference between Second Life and Facebook in that the two platforms are real and not-real in dissimilar ways. Facebook provides an opportunity for people to communicate with others, so-called 'real selves', represented by real images and, in the words of one student interviewed, 'generally you know them; it's the real person'. However, the sense of a shared physical space in which these 'real selves' communicate is absent. In a virtual world, although a person operating an avatar has a physical reality, this is not directly who you see, and the images represented there are simulacral rather than real. Virtual worlds recreate the dynamics and spatiality of physical reality in a way that Facebook and its equivalents do not. Both online environments therefore have advantages and disadvantages from the perspective of this user. But it is also clear that both the simulacral nature and the spatial element of a 3D digital space require engagement of belief to be completely effective, which is not always forthcoming and depends on a range of elements and interactions.

To Activity Theory and beyond

The interactions that take place in any activity are dependent on a range of interrelated factors, which means that making sense of them is a complex process. Reducing these separate elements to a manageable and discrete set of characteristics could be treated as reductionist. However, in many cases of high complexity a degree of reductionism can be a practical first step. Activity Theory has probably the greatest 'notion of historicity' than other attempts at such approximations (Masterman, 2008: 212). The basis of Activity Theory is that an activity can be represented as the action of a subject on an object, but this will always be mediated through the employment of an external artefact. This viewpoint draws chiefly on the work of a Russian psychologist, Lev Vygotsky, in the 1920s (Edwards, 2004: 88–9). One of his collaborators, Aleksei Leont'ev, represented this in diagrammatic form, as shown in Figure 5.1 (ibid.: 89):

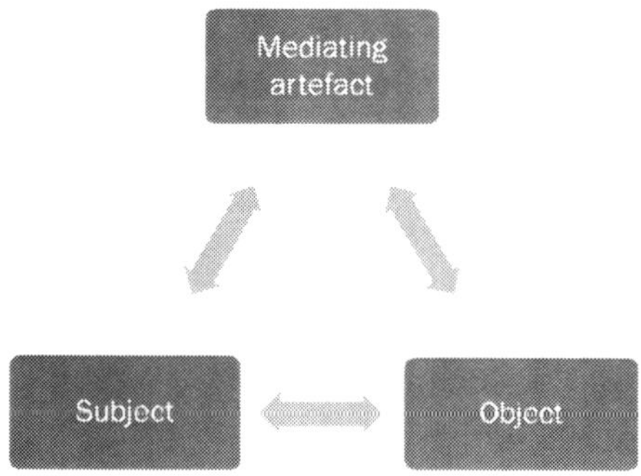

Figure 5.1 **The basis of Activity Theory**

The 'subject' here is the individual (or group) or, in other words, an active agent in the activity, and the 'object' refers to the 'raw material' or 'problem space' or the focus of the activity. The mediating artefacts can be the language or tools participants use, or a technological platform such as a learning management system or a virtual world. In the 1990s, Yrjö Engeström developed this idea further by not only considering the contexts in which this triad is placed, but also by reflecting on 'the dynamic relationships that exist within settings between, for example, traditions, responsibilities, how resources are used and the outcomes of interactions' (ibid.). These contexts are separated into three different categories and represented in Figure 5.2 below:

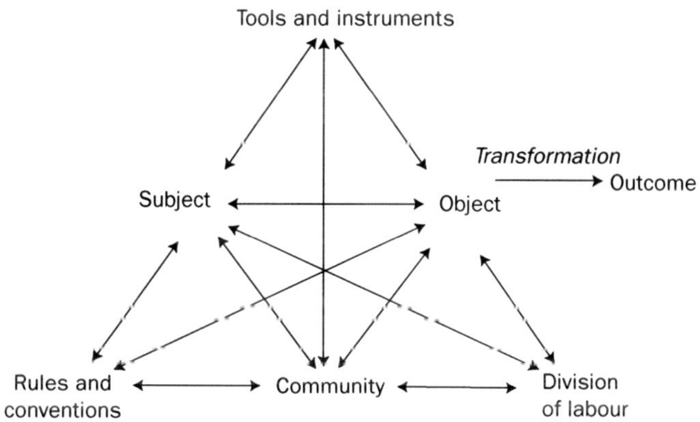

Figure 5.2 **The essential elements of Activity Theory and their interrelationships**

Source: image author's own; adapted from Engeström, 1987

The strength of Activity Theory is that it can be applied as a cross-disciplinary framework with 'both individual and social levels linked at the same time' (Masterman, 2008: 212). An individual study can also reduce the number of categories to focus on any dyadic relationship between constituent parts. A weakness, however, could be seen in representing the elements of Activity Theory by a geometrical diagram, implying that the factors influencing the outcome are discrete and static. This is not the case. The intention is to simply represent these factors and indicate how they are connected. These connections, however, may be constantly changing, open to external influence and waxing and waning in their relative importance and dominance. A more telling omission is that Activity Theory does not take into account the essential aspect of experience discussed in this chapter – the relationship with the space (in this case a virtual one) in which the activity is located.

The Communities of Practice model (Figure 5.3) is a framework for describing the process by which an individual's participation in a community can develop, and the ways in which the community itself can evolve (Wenger, 1998: 149). As with Activity Theory, its value as an

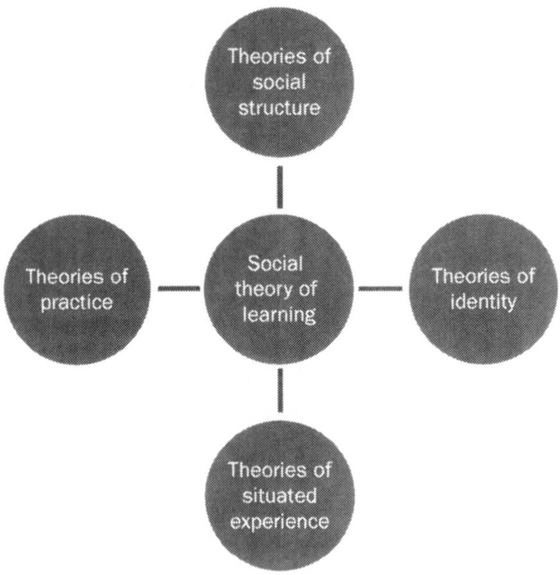

Figure 5.3 **Relationships of various theoretical traditions within the Communities of Practice model**

Source: image author's own; adapted from Wenger, 1998: 12

analytical tool is that it reduces a complex set of interrelated factors to simpler components and incorporates other theories, including social structure and theories of practice. In so doing, this model takes into account situated experience and identity.

This overview, however, is lacking when considering the tools and artefacts that mediate the community interactions addressed by the Activity Theory model. To address this, an extended version of Activity Theory is proposed. Categories such as situated experience (labelled as 'presence' and equivalent to psychological immersion) and identity are added as additional points to act as a mash-up of the Activity Theory and Communities of Practice models described above. To maintain the interconnectedness of all the factors, these two new categories are placed above and below the plane on which the diagram in Figure 5.2 is drawn. Finally, as an aesthetic touch, the vertices are all made the same length to produce the cube below (Figure 5.4). This model (described in more detail in Childs, 2010) is employed as the framework for analysing the constituent elements of the particular type of spaces discussed in the following two chapters. These are not only virtual spaces but are also a range of physical spaces that require an engagement of belief to give them their unique character.

The Communities of Practice model is also connected to the discussion below in that the model uses a spatial metaphor in some of its

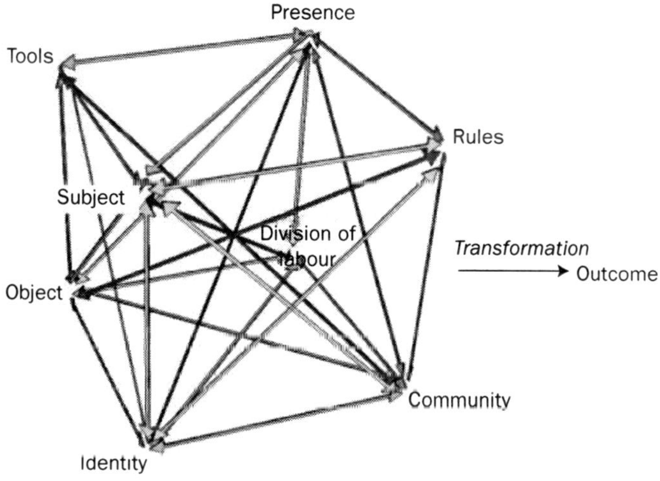

Figure 5.4 **An extended Activity Theory model, incorporating situated experience ('presence') and identity**

categorizations, describing the types of participation with a community in terms of different trajectories that can be inbound (becoming more involved in the community), or outbound (becoming less involved). Boundaries are important concepts in the Communities of Practice model since they 'can create divisions and be a source of separation, fragmentation, disconnection, and misunderstanding. Yet, they can also be areas of unusual learning, places where perspectives meet and new possibilities arise' (Wenger, 2000: 233–6). Boundaries require specific processes for people to pass through them, from outside the community to inside, acquiring skills and knowledge (*processes*), learning specific languages (*discourses*) and even acquiring specialist tools, documents or equipment (*artefacts*) in order to transit them, all described as *boundary objects*. These complex activities can be aided by making the processes transparent, as well as by appointing brokers for the community to 'span the boundaries' (ibid.).

Notes

1. *http://www.schome.ac.uk/.*
2. *http://cms.cch.kcl.ac.uk/theatron/.*

6

Other spaces, and other ways of making sense of them

Abstract: This chapter builds upon the idea of virtual spaces requiring an engagement of belief in order for the participant to be fully engaged with them. The concepts of semiotic social spaces, magic circles, game spheres and lusory attitude are introduced, and the similarities and complementarities of these ideas applicable to a variety of spaces (virtual worlds, theatrical spaces, games and ritual spaces) are explored. Metaxis, engagement, immersion and how these contribute to flow are also discussed. Furthermore, the chapter introduces the third set of concepts, those of crossing over between spaces, which include the idea of liminality, or a membrane. It concludes with a discussion of the concept of a dichotomy between apparent and actual intent in crossing into a game sphere.

Key words: engagement of belief, semiotic social spaces, magic circles, game spheres, lusory attitude, metaxis, engagement, immersion, flow, liminality, membrane, prelusory goal.

Entering into a world of make-believe

Virtual worlds fall into a special category of space. They require the engagement of belief and the particular intention of people within them to fully define them as such. This type of space, however, is not unique to the virtual world, and a range of models used to describe it are examined below.

The first of these models was developed by James Paul Gee as a counter to Wenger's idea of Communities of Practice. Whereas Wenger uses space as a metaphor, Gee, in his concept of *affinity spaces*, refers to literal spaces, and how they can be used to understand the ways in which groups of people work together. Instead of viewing people as being unified by their relationship to each other, they are looked at in terms of being unified by a common endeavour taking place in the same space (Gee, 2005: 214, 216). Although what Gee terms affinity spaces are the focus of his interest, these are really just examples of a wider categorization he has identified, that of the semiotic social space (SSS), and it is this concept that the following discussion will examine in particular. SSSes are not just physical spaces – they can be a website, a chatroom or a virtual world. What makes an SSS different from any other type of non-social, non-semiotic space is that there is an intention behind its development and the rationale for being within it (ibid.: 218). This could be a game, which people choose to play, or a classroom, which people are sent to learn in, or a pub, in which people go to socialize. Gee identified two sets of signifying systems associated with the space:

1. an internal system (the content and structure of the space); and
2. an external system (the social practices and the wider consequences of the existence of the space).

So, for example, the internal semiotic structure of a game would consist of its rules, the level design, the character interactions, and so on; whereas the external 'grammar' would include discussions about the game in forums, reviews and debates in the media (ibid.: 219–20).

Another essential part of the SSS is the idea of a portal – an intermediate space – in which the internal signifying system of the full SSS can be accessed before the actual environment. This has many similarities to Wenger's idea of a boundary, though Gee emphasizes that this is literally a portal to an actual space, not a metaphorical boundary. As mentioned above, where the SSS plays host to a form of unified action it becomes an affinity space (ibid.: 225). By examining the particular example of an online gaming site, Gee states that this common endeavour transcends differences in ethnicity, gender, ability, or class and that all share the same environment regardless of their experience (though with the choice to be segregated to some extent if needed). From a practical perspective of analysing how people work with one another, Gee's model has advantages over Wenger's in that it can be applied when participants are not tied together by a shared sense of practice and of community, but simply by sharing a space. Gee's analysis adds most to the debate about space and sense-making, because it draws specifically on the idea of spaces being semiotic signifying systems, in addition to a location for people to act together.

The degree to which this system has an impact on how sense is made of the space is greater for some spaces than others. For example, an academically able student and a less able student may experience different emotions when entering a school, but the elements of the school generally have the same meaning. Environments that have a great deal of symbolic meaning for one person may have very little for another, and so fail to be understood; an example being the religious iconography within a church or cathedral. Semiotic spaces are also demarcated by the specialist use of language. For example, in order to play *World of Warcraft* for the first time, it is necessary to understand the differences between class and trade skills and to make sense of such words as 'buff' or 'tank' (which are used in a completely different way outside of the game). This could be quite an alienating process. But once the player is accustomed to the rules and the jargon, their sense of belonging to that environment is redefined. Although Gee would state that the same affinity space is shared by both newbies and masters, the fact that higher-level players will be more aware of a wider range of discourses (to draw on Wenger's model) means that they are extracting different meanings from the signifying system around them than lower-level players. They may occupy the same game environment, but from a post-structuralist perspective they inhabit a very different semiotic space.

Another way of conceptualizing types of spaces is the idea of space being a magic circle or play sphere. In 1938, Johan Huizinga raised the idea of the magic circle as a way to describe a game environment as a separate self-contained space. While the game is being played, its goals, ambitions, purpose and activities are governed by a different set of rules and conventions than in real life. A game may consist of 'a literal physical precinct: a chessboard, ring, arena, field, stadium, stage, altar, etc. There are also sharp temporal boundaries, a clear beginning and an end, which clearly mark the game off as a temporary interruption of ordinary life' (Rodriguez, 2006). For example, when playing the board game *Monopoly* (published by Hasbro), value is attached to the acquisition of properties and of play money. All participants are aware that the money has no intrinsic value; it only has meaning within the rules and conventions of the play space, comprised of the board and the space around the players. Yet for the duration of the play, acquiring money is important, because it is the scoring system by which the game may be won or lost. This awareness of the wider context is suppressed, in order for the game to have merit; the awareness is there but the players engage in a willing suspension of disbelief. This separate and discrete space is also a consequence-free environment, in which people can practise different behaviours without repercussions in the wider world; a specific form of Erikson's notion of a psychosocial moratorium (Begg et al., 2007).

Roger Caillois echoes the idea of a game space being separate and self-contained, with its own rules, and requiring a willing engagement of belief in its conventions. This is 'the temporary acceptance, if not of an illusion ... then at least of a closed, conventional, and, in certain respects, imaginary universe' (Caillois, 1961: 19). All games, Caillois claims, have an element of make-believe 'accompanied by a special awareness of a second reality or of a free unreality, as against real life' and indeed the entire purpose of play presupposes this (ibid.: 9–10). Bernard Suits refers to this as a 'lusory attitude' that is 'the acceptance of constitutive rules just so the activity made possible by such an acceptance can occur' (Suits, 2005: 54). Without this acceptance of the rules constraining activity, without this shared belief that the aimed-for goal matters, and without this striving to compete or overcome the challenge, the whole purpose of actually taking part in the game is absent.

Neither here nor there – the state of metaxis

The idea above of a self-contained space also has parallels in film studies, in which the world of the film is considered as a self-consistent 'story world' or 'internal representational world' (de Freitas and Oliver, 2006: 252) and extends beyond the immediate text or what is seen on the screen. This conception of a consistent separate world is called the story's diegesis and can include back stories, characters' motivations and what may (or may not) be occurring out of shot, or between sequences. The 'diegetic effect' is a submersion within the fictional world and also requires a willing suspension of disbelief, (or, to use Heeter's refinement of the phrase, an 'engagement of belief'). The viewer becomes immersed in this fiction and can strongly identify with the experiences of the people on the screen. This immersion, however, is not necessarily complete. Although while a film runs, the story world is entered and the experiences can feel real, we are still aware that the world is a constructed artificiality ('it's only a movie'). Furthermore, as with the idea of 'arrival' and 'departure' discussed earlier, immersion in the story world (or distancing from it) is not an either/or state, nor it is static. One can alternate between them, or experience a divided self, split between the two states.

One moment the viewer can be analysing the film, recognizing actors and placing which films they have been in before, and the next, they are caught up in the action or drama.

In gaming, this distinction has been described by Diane Carr as a difference between engagement and immersion – two of the three essential aspects of game-playing (Carr, 2006: 55). Engagement, in this context, is when the player adopts a critical reflective stance outside of the game (a term Carr borrows from literature studies). Carr's use of immersion is in the same sense as that of psychological immersion applied throughout this discussion. She notes that the absorption into the world that occurs when immersion takes place is seen as an uncritical position associated with undemanding literature; whereas engagement requires interpretive skills and external referents. Carr therefore considers both immersion and engagement as being important parts of interaction with games, and states that they are mutually dependent. It is when a player moves constantly between these two states that the game is at its most compelling (ibid.). This alternation also gives rise to 'flow' (which according to Carr is the third essential aspect of games) – a concept originated by Mihaly Csíkszentmihályi describing a state in which attention is heightened, and where goals, action and the environment are all aligned. It is an optimal experience, which is both enjoyable and productive. For example, for games to possess *flow*, they must retain the following characteristics: be a challenging activity requiring concentration and the application of skills, merge action and awareness through clear attainable goals and immediate feedback, provide an illusion of control (in that one controls the actions, but those actions are predetermined by the game's designers), encourage a loss of self-consciousness, and transform the sense of the passage of time (Järvinen et al., 2002: 20–1).

In education, this ability to switch between the two states provides additional opportunities for learning, as argued by a number of educationalists. Sara de Freitas and Martin Oliver refer to the entry into the world of simulation, combined with taking a critical stance and reflecting on the process of immersion, as 'double identification'. They state that '[T]his "double" identification approach to the game may in part explain why the use of "other worlds" can indeed accelerate learning, allowing the learner to at once participate within the "world" and to reflect upon their relationship when viewed from outside of it' (2006: 255). For example, in the Teatrix virtual world (Machado et al., 2001: 6) children have avatars based on the *Little Red Riding Hood* story. After role-playing within the world, young learners reflect on the interaction, drawing on their knowledge of the characters' background and emotions that exist beyond the immediate contact that took place. This gives them the opportunity to explore different attitudes and behaviours, both by relating closely with the character, then stepping out of the narrative and discussing the character's motivations. Thus the narrative learning environment formally constructs the interior and the exterior grammar of the learning activity, which is used interchangeably. This switching between states of critical engagement and immersion is also an acknowledged part of performance studies and occurs when actors go 'in and out of role between imaginary worlds and the here-and-now' (McGeoch and Hughes, 2009: 125). The term employed to describe this alternating or divided state is metaxis.

In *Homo Ludens*, Johan Huizinga applies the concept of the magic circle to rituals and religious spaces, where the same double identification takes place. He notes the unlikelihood of the conviction that people have in the various creation myths, and sees them as poetic metaphors indistinguishable from the conception of celestial beings in theology (Huizinga, 1970: 163). He cites, as his examples, medieval theologians Alain de Lille and Hildegard of Bingen, both discussing theological matters about their beliefs. While doing so, the former is still 'fully aware of the imaginary character of his apparatus' and the latter lays 'no claim to the metaphysical reality of the Virtues that she sees in her visions'. Huizinga refers to these forms of discourse that cross over between 'fancy and conviction' as play elements. With specific reference to theriomorphism in many early religions, Huizinga claims that 'the theriomorphic factor in ritual, mythology and religion can best be understood in terms of the play attitude' (ibid.: 164–5). The participants in these religions enter a play sphere in which the 'sacred representation of man as an animal was perfectly "serious"' (ibid.). Huizinga is claiming, therefore, that medieval views of religious belief were rules and conventions that existed apart from the real world and reality and faith (as in a form of metaxis) could be maintained simultaneously.

Passing between: crossing the threshold between realities

The above link between play and ritual has also been noted by cultural anthropologist Victor Turner, who paid particular attention to the crossing over between the internal and the external spaces that Gee refers to. Richard Schechner, a frequent collaborator of Turner (Schechner, 2006: 16–17) provides a summary of Turner's extensive work; most relevant to this discussion is Schechner's analysis of Turner's 1969 book, *The Ritual Process: Structure and Anti-Structure*. Instead of Gee's use of the word portal (or Wenger's use of boundary) Turner drew on the idea of the *limen*, which is the thin strip between the inside and outside of a building or room which links the two spaces. Historically, the limen demarcates the edge of a stage, separating the imaginary world of the actors from the audience. Ritually, it still has significance in traditions such as the first time a bride enters the matrimonial house and is carried across the threshold by her husband; since she does not step across herself this constitutes a discontinuity between her identity before marriage and her new identity as a wife. Turner described those between-spaces as *liminal*, but notes that liminality could also be temporal (not just spatial), for example in the moments during which a regular space is transformed into a sacred one through a ritual process. Furthermore, this liminal time has two stages:

1. the moment when participants have their outside world identities and status removed and therefore become powerless and open to change; and
2. when they have their new identities written onto them and are initiated into their new roles and positions.

Once this liminal phase is concluded, what participants do and the objects with which they interact assume and project much greater significance than their practical use or value, or even their outer-world significance (Schechner, 2006: 17, 66–7). To adopt Gee's (and role-playing games') terminologies, once the liminal phase is completed the semiotic signifying system of the social space has levelled up. Once in their new identities that are created by passing the liminal moment or space, people are removed from the constraints and demands of their regular lives. This enables them to feel consumed by their new roles, and transformed and liberated by them. This may not be consequence-free, but they are subject to differing rules and conventions. For example, one may not give oneself over to speaking in tongues or ecstatic dancing while at the supermarket but within many congregations it is perfectly acceptable. Turner's phrase for this is 'anti-structure' (Schechner, 2006: 70) and is similar to the description of the psychosocial moratorium that is implicit in the concept of the magic circle and of flow. He extends this idea further to state that such freeing of the constraints of normal life provides the opportunity for social and personal differences to be set aside, resulting in a greater feeling of unity, which can occur in secular and sacred spaces. This state is referred to as *communitas*, which in turn could be normative (structured and imposed) – arising, for example, during the shared singing and praying in a church service – and also spontaneous, when there is a shared deep affinity between participants and unified action. The latter could happen within a theatre play, on a sports field (not just between the players, but also the fans), or between Guild members in *World of Warcraft* when conducting a successful raid. Turner identifies similar processes happening in a range of other types of spaces associated with the arts and entertainment that were ritual-like and standardized, but voluntary, and more playful. These he described as 'liminoid'. Actors' warm-up exercises, the use of music to signify the start of a show, and people's own personal rituals before engaging in a performance, all help define the transition of an area from being a simple stage to a site in which this creative action takes place. Turner also describes post-performance liminoid activities, in which the space returns to the ordinary, and includes in these 'cooling down' ritualized behaviour and post-performance suppers (Schechner, 2006: 67, 69).

Edward Castronova, in discussing Huizinga's magic circle, describes the boundary around it as a membrane (2005: 147). Although he acknowledges that the rules are quite different inside and outside the circle, he also notes that the membrane is quite porous, and that people carry their 'behavioural assumptions and attitudes with them' (ibid.). Castronova argues this primarily in an economic sense – so, because things have importance within the play sphere, they also have the potential to gain value outside of it. For example, if the amount of money with which one could start a game of *Monopoly* was held over from game to game, then to gain an advantage, players may be driven to purchase it outside of the play sphere (giving rise to the real money trading that Castronova discusses). The play money would therefore acquire real economic value and the distinction between virtual and real would break down. In the context of a board game, this may not seem plausible, but where a virtual world is concerned – which is persistent and shared by many people, and where status is attained through the purchasing of virtual content – then the movement of value across the membrane is almost inevitable. For example, within Second Life members of vampire communities gain status by the number of 'souls' they acquire and the amount of 'blood' they consume by feeding on non-vampires. Although intended as a feature enhancing role-playing, this has led to a black market in the selling of souls and blood outside of the game so that members of the vampire community can obtain higher status. This, in turn, has led to people acquiring real money through harvesting 'blood' from unsuspecting newbies and selling this to role-playing vampires, leading in turn to inworld warnings against the activities of these so-called 'spampires'.

The difficulty some commentators have with Castronova's position is that this porosity is not simply limited to the transfer of value in virtual worlds, it occurs across the boundary of any magic circle, for a wide range of reasons. Castronova states that '[T]he membrane can be considered a shield of sorts, protecting the fantasy world from the outside world. The inner world needs defining and protecting because it is necessary that everyone who goes there adheres to a specific set of inside rules' (ibid.). The shield also works to protect and enable particular behaviours in the fantasy world, so that if a participant behaves insanely in the membrane this will not have an impact in the larger world. In reality, the boundary between the internal play space and the external world is not a solid one, and the play sphere is neither shielded from the external effects nor is what happens within a game entirely free of consequence. This porosity across the boundaries of a magic circle is also at the root of why some take issue with the concept of the magic circle itself. For example, John Carter McKnight argues in his blog post:

> [T]here is not a game that isn't subject to a broad range of customs, norms, cultural assumptions, administrative regulations and national laws. You cannot think usefully about games apart from the culture of their creators and players ... the magic circle sees games/plays not as deeply embedded in culture, but indeed apart, at best a culture unto themselves, at worst, too trivial to merit rigorous analysis.
>
> (McKnight, 2011)

To illustrate the argument above and to demonstrate the degree to which these two worlds (inside and outside the magic circle) are both independent and dependent on each other, the example of *Monopoly* can again be drawn upon. Although during the game the players' goal is to accumulate play money, this belief in the value of these make-believe British pounds, US dollars or Coruscant credits (depending on the edition) ends outside of the game. Despite this, the links between the outside and inside worlds are still strong. *Monopoly* was originally an educational tool to demonstrate the inequity of owning land, known as *The Landlord's Game* (Ettlinger, 2009: 92). Therefore, its design and origins are not an isolated sphere separated from the rest of the world, but spring directly out of the political and economic concerns of the Georgist movement of the 1900s. On the other hand, its later pro-capitalism modification does little to change the experience of playing it as a game, as Ettlinger states '[O]ur game of *Monopoly* was as much about friendship as capitalism; as much about compassion as ruthlessness; and as much about contingency as path dependence' (ibid.). Within the play sphere, it is still just a game, and to enjoy playing it does not require one to be a capitalist; the normal social conventions of charity, compassion and altruism (that one would hope we all share) can be suspended for the purposes of ensuring the game is enjoyable. To assume that the game space provides an entirely consequence-free psychosocial moratorium is also questionable, to which anyone who has had to endure the recriminations and bad tempers after playing a particularly competitive round of *Monopoly* with friends or family can attest. The play sphere is indeed detached from the surrounding environment with its own rules and conventions; just not *that* detached.

More spin on the concept: the dichotomy between apparent and actual intent

Nancy Ettlinger raises another key point about the aims of game-playing. She argues that in *Monopoly* the goal to attain the most money (or property) is merely arbitrary. It is adopted to set a competition, in order to have a basis for playing. This mismatch between apparent and actual goals is a key factor in the understanding of games. To explain this, Bernard Suits draws on the example of a high-jumper (Suits, 2005: 93). In high-jumping, the aim appears to be to get over to the other side of the bar. Suits calls this a prelusory goal, in that it only makes sense from the viewpoint of the external grammar of the game (ibid.: 51). However, there is a range of ways to get there without jumping over the bar, one could simply walk beneath it, for example. A set of constraints and requirements are put in place to make this goal harder to achieve, so that when it is accomplished, the jumper feels a sense of success, and the audience can share the experience together with them. Though achieving the prelusory goal appears to be the aim, this actually has no real value in itself. It is the transforming effect that occurs when the other side is reached through overcoming obstacles that is the actual goal; a spin on apparent and actual intent to which Suits refers as 'reverse English' (ibid.: 93). Not all games are played solely for the intrinsic merit of just playing. They may also be played in order to earn money, or in order to impress someone, or to keep people happy (all categories of participant that Suits describes as 'professionals' [ibid.: 130]). Despite the fact that those participants have a different attitude towards playing the game, they still accept its goals, rules and constraints, 'just because such acceptance makes such activity possible' (ibid.: 131). In other words, this still requires an engagement of belief in the different conventions of the space in order for the activity to take place irrespective of the ultimate purpose.

The interaction with other forms of spaces also has the potential for this seeming displacement between apparent and actual intent. Although the structure of narrative drives the audience towards a resolution (or solution), this is not why we enjoy it; otherwise we would just read the last page. It is the departure from our daily lives and arrival at a transformed sense of self that is the goal, which is shared with others. Likewise with public ritual spaces – although worship of a divine being may be the purpose for some, this can be done in private. It is the sense of communitas that occurs when rituals are conducted among others and the opportunity to leave daily identities at the door that draws people to such spaces, hence simple attendance is insufficient. The manifestation of (or at least pretence of) belief in the rituals is also required for the experience of communitas, which is the true goal of the activity. Finally, and most relevant to this discussion, when entering a virtual world the participant may be doing it solely for the pleasure of exploring the space, or in order to take part in a learning action, but without engaging belief in the space neither form of activity will be carried out effectively. This is due to the relationship between emotional engagement and the experience of space and cognition, and is explored more thoroughly below.

In summary, many writers have identified the existence of spaces that provide a location in which we can transcend our normal everyday lives, whether they are for play, for ritual, for performance, or for engaging with stories or virtual worlds. These places all require the engagement of belief by those who enter them for their full nature to be realized. One of the more enduring labels for these places is Huizinga's conception of the magic circle, but although in its original definition this does not actually imply the complete separation of the play sphere from the rest of culture, this now tends to be what the term connotes among many people studying such spaces (McKnight, 2012). This general view of the term makes employing it without these connotations problematic. The following chapter attempts to establish a terminology to identify and discuss these types of spaces, focusing on inventing some new labels, merging the models analysed above – but without the connotation that these spaces are shielded and detached from the rest of the world.

7

First, second, third and fourth places – making extra sense of space

Abstract: This chapter introduces and describes the idea of first, second and third places. It elaborates on the discussion in the preceding chapter of there being a set of spaces in which engagement of belief is integral to sense-making within them, and brings it into a single coherent frame through the introduction of the concept of a 'fourth place'. The characteristics of fourth places are delineated using the framework of extended Activity Theory proposed in Chapter 5. In fourth places, the situated experience of the space is characterized by an engagement of belief, and an experience of metaxis, a splitting of awareness into apparent and actual intent. The tools of this engagement are a set of boundary objects and practices that mark the space as a highly structured semiotic space. These spaces are also specifically 'about' something, and this aligns both their design and the intent of the people that enter them. Both rules governing behaviour and the roles of participants are transformed by entry to these spaces, and this transformation is both legitimized by the space and by the rationale for entering the space. A sense of shared community also typifies these spaces. The concept of a fourth place is thus presented here as a novel way to classify the type of space, which both draws together the strengths of previous ways of characterizing spaces and also normalizes them as an extension of other places with which we are familiar.

Key words: first place, second place, third place, presence, Communities of Practice, engagement of belief, extended Activity Theory, semiotic social spaces, magic circles, game spheres, metaxis, engagement, liminality, membrane, fourth place.

In the opening paragraphs of Chapter 5, the Schome Initiative was introduced as an online space for interaction which was neither school nor home. In essence, combining these two types of spaces is ambitious and complex, in that school and home each belongs to a very different type of space. A typology for describing these types of spaces was suggested by Oldenburg and Brissett who noted that American life was being reduced to 'a very restrictive two-stop model of daily existence, the office or shop and the home, joined by the ordeal of commuting' with few opportunities for social participation (1982: 266). They proposed a typology consisting of first places (an individual's home), second places (the workplace) and third places (personalizable and informal public gathering spaces), which they referred to as 'great good places'. Third places generally have a clear set of attributes in that they are highly accessible, welcoming and comfortable; they involve regular participants and provide for both old and new friendships (Peachey, 2010: 104). Although Oldenburg and Brissett's argument is couched in terms of social malaise and a decline in moral standards (1982: 265), and nostalgically harks back to a golden age when these 'great good places' were the heart of a community's social vitality (Peachey, 2010: 104), the typology has proved to be a very useful one with which to describe these different types of spaces. Their definition, however, is not always uncontested. As Gee (2005: 225) states, spaces that are 'about something' have a semiotic structure, and the view of them will therefore depend to some extent on the meaning ascribed to them by the individual. School is very clearly akin to a workplace for most children and therefore a second place, but there is a strong social element to attendance, and some locations within the school may become defined as third places (such as unused staircases or behind the bike sheds). Similarly, entire locations may be assigned different meanings entirely due to one's own perspective. For an active and fit person, a gym may be a third place in that it provides an opportunity to socialize, it is accessible, comfortable and enjoyable. For an unfit person who feels compelled to attend one in order to stave off some of the more debilitating effects of encroaching middle age, gymnasia are definitely second places.

The predominant third places that exist in the twenty-first century are evidently the online spaces that have been created through social networking sites such as Facebook and Twitter. Constance Steinkuehler argues that massive multi-player online games also fulfil the requirement of a third place (2005: 17). She uses *Lineage* as an example of this, describing it as a neutral space that enables socialization and personalization, but being neither a work- or home-like environment. It has already been discussed in this part of the book that in order to take full effect of virtual spaces, the user is required to engage their *belief* in order to cross the threshold from the physical to the virtual. This could be described as 'crossing the membrane' or entering the magic circle, but these terms are somewhat problematic for many researchers. Therefore, it is proposed here to extend Oldenburg and Brisset's typology to define spaces that require suspension of disbelief in order to participate as 'fourth places'.

The idea of a 'fourth place' also extends to the physical world, as an umbrella term for the story world, ritual and game spaces discussed in the previous chapter. Unlike the usual formulation of the term 'magic circle', these spaces are not separated from first, second and third places any more than home life is shielded from what happens at work, or than an evening out in a nightclub has no effect on one's work the next morning. Who we are, and what we are, can be carried across the threshold into a fourth place if we so choose; we can alter that identity and allow that space to exert a psychosocial moratorium for the duration of our stay there.

First, second and third places are semiotic social spaces, but the role that semiotics plays within a fourth place is particularly significant. There is a range of characteristics which are heightened within fourth places, although not specific to them. Taking the extended Activity Theory model as a lattice, the separate elements of spaces described by the writers in this part of the book can be structured into a single set of criteria as follows:

- *Belief and metaxis (presence).* The subjects are required to suspend disbelief, or, more exactly, engage belief, in the space to fully experience the sense of location within it. This belief is fostered through emotional experiences and through an intentionality, or 'lusory attitude', in both the design of the space and the purpose of the person entering it. This requirement of belief can result in the experience of the space by one who engages in this way being markedly different from that of one who does not. The experience of the external world may not be entirely suspended when a participant enters a virtual world, leading to a division in awareness or consciousness. This splitting of awareness may occur, for example, in ritual spaces (one is aware that there is a physical material universe that obeys laws of cause and effect even when one engages in religious belief) and in games (one is aware that ultimately the process of scoring a goal – for example – has no objective value, but the awareness of this is suspended during the game itself for the purpose of enjoying it). In theatre, cinema and literature, the diegetic effect, in which immersion takes place, can be concurrent with critical reflection leading to a 'double identification' of engagement and immersion. Switching between the two phases of this double identification can also provide more opportunities to experience 'flow'.

- *Boundary objects and semiotics (tools).* These spaces are often mediated through specialist language, objects and practices. Users may invent words to describe objects and activities that take place within them, or they may appropriate words and use them with different meanings. Understanding and using these terms are examples of boundary objects that are part of the induction into the community that uses the space. The spaces often use artefacts that can only be found within them, and which new participants must obtain in order to become fully active participants in that space. Acquisition of these boundary objects is also a marker of status within the community – for example, particular accessories that are accessible only at particular levels in *World of Warcraft,* or objects that are passed freely from person to person but which require some interaction with others to obtain, such as the flight feathers in Second Life. The spaces are particularly dense in connotation which marks them as very different experiences for those entering into them, depending on the degree to which they decode the signifying system. The internal grammar of a space may be quite different from its external grammar, and the semiotic system may ascribe a more heightened degree of meaning and symbolism to objects and the participants' ability to interpret them. These skills develop over time, identifying the user as part of the community.
- *Different goals and aims (object).* Fourth places are 'about something' to use Gee's phrase above. However, for a shared agreement on their purpose to be maintained there is a requirement of the engagement of belief in a set of goals. Unlike other spaces, such as school or work, which have generally agreed measures of success within the wider world, the goals within fourth places only have value if a set of conventions specific to that space is adopted. Often, these conventions only persist while within the play sphere of the fourth place; though they may extend beyond it if the rules and conventions of the play sphere are adopted. This is Huizinga's so-called magic circle (Huizinga, 1970), but fourth places acknowledge the significant porosity in the membrane that bounds the space – in that status, value or beliefs translate or can be converted to exterior spaces.
- *Transformation of role and status (division of labour).* In crossing over to a fourth place, identity and status are transformed, one role is

removed and another may be assigned. A person with little status in the exterior world may be an elder within a church, or may become a 30th level paladin or a monopolistic landlord. Within the communities in the fourth places, brokers have high status and a key role in that they act as boundary spanners to help induct new people to the processes of the space. Furthermore, irrespective of status in the external world, the newcomer to the space will become a newb, or, worse, a noob, in their first entries, finding their old identity erased but not yet having formed a new one. These initial experiences may be seen to be marginal or peripheral and may lead to different trajectories through the community.

- *Suspension of normal conventions, transformation of time (rules).* The space could encapsulate different conventions and different roles for participants. Although the crossover between the spaces (real and virtual) is not negligible there is a psychosocial moratorium on many behaviours, and the normal awareness of time may not be as strong. Fourth places are rarely an entirely consequence-free environment, but usually different behaviours and activities are permitted in a form of 'anti-structure' and this freedom from the constraint of normal daily life permits a heightened sense of experience and belonging.
- *Participation requires the ability to engage belief (subject).* Fourth places, as with third places, tend to be voluntary in their participation. A distinction between the two types of place, however, is that to be fully present within the space requires an act of engagement of belief. We need to take on the rules and conventions of the space sufficiently in order to 'depart' the mundane and literal space surrounding us and, through a volitional act, 'arrive' at a heightened connection to the space surrounding us. All reactions to spaces are subjective. A student may be bored or interested in school, and a workplace may be fulfilling or unfulfilling. The difference a fourth place engenders is that through adopting the semiotic system of the place, by suppressing the perspectives of daily life, the perceptions of the space are significantly altered, as are one's sense of self and of time. For a significant number of people, it may be likely that they are so strongly situated in the physical world and their physical bodies (or are unable to adopt the shared belief system of the space) that a full experience of the space may not be possible. Not everyone can be Peter Pan.
- *Identity and role-play (identity).* One's sense of self may be quite radically altered as one enters a fourth place. If one is an actor on a stage, then one adopts a role for the period of that performance.

A participant in a virtual world may embrace a projective identity, or may actually discover that their personality has changed in the process of adapting to the different affordances of the space. A person's status may also change with the crossing over to the fourth place, due to their role within the community. These are not necessarily absolutely divided; the experience in a fourth place may well have an impact on the experience of the remainder of the participant's life.

- *Community and communitas (community).* Fourth places are 'about something'. They are usually the locus of a specific community that finds its identity and purpose through the coming together within those spaces. As with all the other categories, however, the edges of the space are porous. The community developed within the space may well find expression outside of it, but the nature and experience of that community is markedly different within the fourth place in comparison to outside of it. Also, through the employment of a psychosocial moratorium individuals may feel freer to act and also free from normal social constraints. This can engender a greater feeling of connectedness and 'flow', of normative or spontaneous communitas, particularly as the participants are engaged in a shared activity in which action and awareness become merged.
- *Transformation and outcome.* In Activity Theory the outcome of the activity occurs as a result of a transformation. In fourth places, often the transformation itself (or rather the experiences that occur during a transformed state) *is* the rationale for the activity, though there may be instrumental (rather than intrinsic) reasons for it. The transformation to and from this state occurs at the beginning and cessation of the activity during the liminal phases, which act as points in transition between the external world and the fourth place. For example, in ritual spaces the use of light and music signals a move from the outside world to the inside world, and the identities of participants are suspended before the ritual begins. In virtual environments, the time between logging on and being able to take an active part in the world (as one waits for the world to be rendered on the monitor) is a liminal phase, in which activity is put on hold and new identities take place. In theatre, as one enters the space, the music and any pre-show activity (by ushers etc.) are all part of the process of transition. These take place either in a specific portal, marking the changeover from the external space to the fourth place, or are a liminal time, where a normal space is transformed through a ritualized practice.

The above model presents nothing revolutionary. It simply brings together the writings of Callois, Carr, Castronova, Gee, Huizinga, Suits, Turner, Wenger and others, and structures these according to an extended Activity Theory model. It also adds its concept of space onto Oldenburg and Brisset's typology of first, second and third places to indicate that although these are different types of places they are merely part of the whole range of spaces we inhabit and move between. Fourth places are particularly important for our experiences and our culture; they could also be termed 'zeroth places', since their existence pre dates all other types of place. The earliest settlements of 9500 years ago were thought to have been created not for farming (a second place) nor for habitation (a first place) but to be close to ritual spaces (Hodder and Cessford, 2004: 17). Ritual spaces gave rise to civilization, not the other way around.

In the following chapter, this view of a virtual space as a fourth place will be employed to analyse two case studies concerned with learning and teaching in virtual worlds. This notion will be further applied in Part 4 of this book, where a number of practitioners reflect on their creative practice in order to understand how they use and make sense of space.

8

Virtual worlds in education

Abstract: This chapter looks at two case studies which demonstrate the impact that experience of space has on the performance and learning of students in virtual worlds. The case studies are placed within the context of prevailing attitudes and understanding of virtual worlds' education over the period in which they were conducted. In the first of these case studies, learners were taken on a field visit to a range of theatrical spaces in Second Life. Their experiences are described using the terms defined and clarified in Chapter 1, and demonstrate the importance of engagement of belief (and time inworld to develop this engagement) for creating fully a sense of place within those spaces. The second case study is set within a simulation of a disaster management communication exercise, and indicates that intent and motivation are key factors in creating emotional agency as well as, in this case, realism. Here, too, the distinction between immediacy and immersion is key to understanding the way in which space is made sense of within virtual worlds.

Key words: immersiveness, immersion, immediacy, realism, navigation, translation of spaces, learning, disclosurism, motivation.

The status of virtual worlds c. 2010

John Kirriemuir is a games-in-learning researcher and also the author of *Virtual World Watch*, a series of reports (mostly financed by the Eduserv Foundation) which summarized the usage of virtual worlds in UK higher education between summer 2007 and spring 2012 (Kirriemuir, 2010). The snapshots chart the progress of the use of virtual worlds. At their peak, all but one higher education institution in the UK had some presence in a virtual world, predominantly Second Life, followed by the gradual fragmentation of this single community. The decision to use virtual worlds was rarely part of an institutional strategy, but was more often than not implemented due to the personal interest of a lecturer intrigued by the potential of such spaces for innovative teaching. Over this period, however, the question of 'Do virtual worlds contribute anything worthwhile to education?' was put to rest (answered with an unequivocal 'Yes'), and the question of what they were most effective at contributing, and how they were least effective, began to be detailed. Kirriemuir's work also included reports on measuring the impact on learning, and on the factors that influence the choice of a particular world, and included an overview of the barriers, responses and bewilderment academics often faced when using virtual spaces.[1]

During this period, the authors used virtual worlds as a medium for educating students on a multiple of occasions in a variety of subject disciplines. It is from this range of activities that the two following examples have been selected – the criterion being that both have (as their basis) a use of space and a requirement for the students to engage with the space in order to meet the educational goals. The two examples differ in subject discipline – one being drawn from theatre and performance, and the other from disaster management studies.

Case 8.1 Learning about theatre design in Second Life (with Iryna Kuksa)[2]

Dr Iryna Kuksa was a visiting lecturer at the School of Theatre, Performance and Cultural Policy Studies, University of Warwick, when she developed and taught the Theatre, Design and New Media: Applications and Implications module for the second-year theatre studies undergraduate degree. The module was designed specifically to give students from the mainly theory-based department an opportunity to have a hands-on experience in learning about scenography and theatrical spaces. One of the main overall goals of the course was for students to develop a critical understanding of the complex and dynamic relationship between design, new media technologies and theatre, and their social and cultural values. One of the new media technology platforms she wanted her students to experience was Second Life. In 2008, she invited Mark Childs to collaborate on delivering this part of the course, as she has for several projects since (including, for example, this book). The aim of the specific session presented here was to introduce students to the methods and conceptual models for visual analysis, interpretation and evaluation of theatrical spaces and sets, and to promote their active engagement with virtual environments. Although this was then the subject of Mark's Ph.D., this was the first of the teaching sessions he had been involved with, and so it was formative for many of the ideas that emerged from that study (including Childs and Kuksa, 2009 and Kuksa and Childs, 2010). The session also provided the opportunity to use some of the theatres produced by the Theatron[3] Project team, by placing them in an educational setting.[3]

After a short introduction discussing virtual worlds in general and their use in performance in particular, the 15 students chose pairs in which to work (or rather six pairs and a group of three). Each pair was then assigned an avatar. They were given 20 minutes (out of the total of two hours) to become accustomed to navigating around the environment and become familiar with how to communicate with each other inworld. During this section, the students were given landmarks to four virtual theatres to explore – two of them were translations of theatres from the physical world (Theatron's Theatre of Epidavros [Figure 8.1] and the Metaverse Shakespeare Company's Globe Theatre) and the other two were theatres created specifically for Second Life (the Caledon Gaiety Theatre and the Ballet Pixelle stage). At the end of the practice session students were asked to teleport to these sites in turn to explore them and examine the following research questions:

1. For the sites based on real-life theatres, the students were asked 'What would be the challenges for actors and designers working in the virtual theatre in Second Life?' and 'What do you think are the challenges for actors and designers in the real theatre this model represents?'
2. For the theatres designed specifically for Second Life, the questions were 'How do these theatres/auditoria differ from real life theatrical spaces?' and 'What can you determine from the stage design (and any other surrounding spaces) to be the nature of the performances, and the communities that built the stages?'

The activity culminated in a final plenary at the end of the seminar.

Figure 8.1 **The Theatre of Epidavros in Second Life**

Source: image reproduced with permission of the Theatron[3] Project

With regard to the question of the challenges of performing in Second Life, it was anticipated that the students would debate the difficulties of performing by using an avatar, through analysing their locomotion qualities and through feeling co-present with the audience. The question on the representation of real sites in virtual worlds required participants to experience the sensation of being located in the spaces. For example, the real Theatre of Epidavros is a very large theatre, and so connecting with the audience and making one's performance large enough is a problem; in addition, the size of that space can be intimidating. The question of the differences between theatres created solely for Second Life and translated theatres was intended to alert students to the ways in which the design of such theatres can adapt to the functionality of that world. For example, the ability of avatars to fly means that aerial ballets are a possibility within the Ballet Pixelle stage, and so there is no roof. The question about stage design drew on the students' experience of the semiotics of virtual spaces – that theatrical spaces are a product of the cultures that created them, drawing on, for example, Aronson (2005: 40) who states that '[W]hat distinguishes the theatres of a particular period or culture is the way in which the arrangement of these elements reflects the spatial configuration of the society at large', a perspective of which the students would have been well aware. The intention here was for the students to observe the detail of the space and of the surroundings of the Caledon Gaiety, to note that the design theme was a Steampunk one (a subgenre of science fiction set in a parallel world in which a high-tech Victorian British Empire exists) and hence to draw the conclusion that the theatre was created to support role-play activity with participants from that particular subculture within Second Life.

Even though they were only given 20 minutes, the students managed to acquire all the basic skills required to interact, communicate and animate their avatars, and move and teleport. As predicted, the biggest issues were to do with moving the camera view and manoeuvring. In fact, the students still struggled to manoeuvre their avatars during the exploration activity, indicated by this conversation:

Student A:	Go backstage.
Student B:	Where is everyone?
Student B:	Shall we go backstage from the stage?
Student A:	Maybe jump in the pit see if we can play any instruments. You can turn round and maybe jump in it.
Student B:	Ooh.
Student A:	It's a jump ... forward. Does it not jump forward?
Student B:	Oh we just jumped on the stage.

The biggest difficulty, however, lay in persuading the students to stop the general exploring and playing around (intended at the beginning to make them feel immersed in the environment), and moving them on to the sensible, educational curriculum part of the activity. Even when they could be persuaded to start looking at the theatres this distraction continued, for some participants more than others – illustrated in this exchange between two students, in which one of them is focusing on the questions set while the other's avatar continually dances (see Figure 8.2), and transcribed as:

Figure 8.2 **Dancing in the Caledon Gaiety**

Student A:	I'm going to try some dancing.
Student B:	[reading from worksheet] What do you think the challenges for actors and designers would be in the real theatre this model represents? [pause] Stop dancing.
Student A:	Sorry.

This particular student's dancing continued throughout the whole session. Even during the final discussion it was still an issue. As can be seen, the dialogue that took place inworld contains one comment concerning the subject matter – a reference to the difficulty with navigation – but this is swamped by discussions about one of the avatars dancing, the clothing of a second avatar and a third having teleported into a pillar (Figures 8.3 and 8.4). This sequence finishes with a plea from Iryna to 'at least talk about the subject'. However, although discussions regarding the subject matter are absent, there is still learning occurring. This learning is about the environment and the experience of space within it. Although the Rosa avatar is dancing constantly, the student operating the avatar reveals that she is doing this to explore the sense of being an avatar on the virtual stage, and conducting herself accordingly. By finding a means to engage with the space, she is making it more real to herself. Rather than being distracted, the student attempts to engage her belief in the space.

Figure 8.3 **Distractions in the Theatre of Epidavros**

After the students had been persuaded to 'teleport back to rl [real life]' a final discussion was conducted about their thoughts on virtual worlds as a medium for education, as well as their responses to the questions. There was also a survey taken of the students' familiarity with various technologies (including gaming), their experience of presence and the degree to which they felt it was a valuable learning activity. The discussion revealed several things – chiefly that, when the question about Second Life as a performance medium was discussed, the students had plenty to say. Similar enthusiasm was evoked when they were asked about the actual appearance of the theatres. They picked up on the issues that lag or a limited range of animations may have on an inworld performance; they also saw that the Ballet Pixelle stage was designed for ballets involving flight. With regard to the questions, which required a cultural context to interpret the semiotic structure of the space and a recount of their emotional experience inworld, the students were not aware that these were topics about which one could ask a question. The ideas were completely out of their realm of experience.

Physical world conversation	**Virtual world conversation**
Student B: Ha that's my favourite. Student A: Theatron Turbo just fell out of the sky. Iryna: Still dancing Rosa. She's like a mad person. Student A: Dancing's quite fun. Iryna: She dances and dances. It's like Saturday Night Fever. In background: Oh we're stuck in the wall. In background: Where are you? Me: I'll just give them a couple of minutes of this. Iryna: Yes they're just fooling around now. All the avatars are changing. Background: We're stuck in a wall. Me: Oh yeah that looks uncomfortable. Iryna: She's so boring. Do something else. You're like the most self-obsessed person, you know? Doing her own thing all the time. Student A: It's all part of the dance though you see. Me: Can we quit now and reconvene and chat through what that was like as an experience? Iryna: But now everbody's chatting. Student B: Well what did you think was going to happen? Iryna: I thought we were going to explore theatre spaces. Me: (Laughing) Maybe we just need to turn off the PCs. Iryna: At least talk about the subject.	Theatron Burner: why the hell are you dancing AGAIN? Menthu Minotaur: ok I'm recording ... Theatron Burner: oops Theatron Burner: sorry Theatron Burner: why on earth do you keep dancing Rosa? Menthu Minotaur: ok so how did that go? Theatron Burner: preety well Theatron Burner: navigating is quite hard Menthu Minotaur: how about moving? Theatron Burner: Turbo we like your outfit Theatron Burner: A LOT Theatron Burner: ... Theatron Turbo: you look sexy Menthu Minotaur: ok we should get back to rl now Theatron Burner: thanks, you too Theatron Breen: you have such long legs turbo Rosa Goldrosen: well Rosa Goldrosen: i like dancing Theatron Burner: awesome skirt Theatron Turbo: thnx Theatron Turbo: lol Rosa Goldrosen: because we're on the stage Theatron Burner: it would look better on my bedroom floor Rosa Goldrosen: it feels right Theatron Turbo: lmao Rosa Goldrosen: could do Rosa Goldrosen: how do I teleport back to rl?

Figure 8.4 **Simultaneous discussions about theatres and dancing**

From observing that students were able to answer some of the questions, but not all, it appeared that the feeling of psychological immersion within the environment is not an experience that either occurs or does not occur, but is gradated. The question about the problems and potential of the space as a performance medium actually asked the students to interact with the environment within a context of hypermediacy, not immediacy. The students were critically engaged with the environment (because they were still struggling with it) and psychological and perceptual immersion in the environment was not needed. Observing the design and construction of the theatres also did not require psychological or perceptual immersion, students simply needed to be able to see the models on the screen. However, the ability to form an emotional connection with the virtual space sufficient to be able to answer the question on how it may have *felt* to be a performer in the real spaces those virtual theatres represented was beyond them. They were unprepared even to appreciate that the question could be answered about a virtual experience. The questions on the cultures were even further beyond the experience they had at that stage. Greater familiarity with the world of Second Life and the separate cultures that exist within it may have made the students more aware of the place of role-play communities within the world. A shared cultural background with the creators of the role-play areas (in this instance, a familiarity with the Steampunk genre) would also have aided a reading of the space, and when this exercise was replicated with people who had several years' experience of being a resident of Second Life, this proved to be the case.

However, from the survey conducted of the students it did appear that most of them had felt psychologically immersed in the environment at least to some extent. This was a small sample size so absolute declarations about the findings weren't possible at the time (though most of these have been confirmed by many follow-up studies).[4] One of the findings was that there was no correlation between whether the students had felt psychologically immersed and their previous experience of technology, though there was a difference due to whether they were gamers or not. Not all of the non-gamers felt immersion, but all of the gamers did. This is probably not unexpected, since part of the fun of playing a game is the ability to feel psychologically immersed in it while it is being played. However, what was surprising was that the same number of students who were non-gamers had problems with navigation, and this was the same proportion as the gamers (about half). In other words, the experience of navigating the game worlds gained by those gaming students did not translate to navigating a virtual world (though it wasn't a hindrance either). Another surprise was that the ease (or difficulty) of navigation was not a factor in whether students found virtual worlds a positive or negative experience; whether they felt psychologically immersed or not, it was still more or less a fifty-fifty split as to whether they mastered the navigation. Again we see the disconnection between immediacy and perceptual and psychological immersion, in that although some of the students were still at a stage where the technology was foregrounded – and struggled to manipulate it – their sense of submersion within the environment was still sufficient for psychological immersion to have taken place. By contrast, some students who had mastered the technology (and so it would be less visible to them) still did not feel part of the world. For an educator, however, the most important discovery was that there was a direct one-to-one correlation between whether the students rated the experience as a valuable learning exercise and whether they felt psychologically immersed.

Each time questions about psychological immersion and learning have been asked of students, in this and other studies since, the same correlation is found (with only one or two exceptions). It is so strong that it can be (almost) absolutely stated that *if a student feels psychologically immersed in the virtual world they will have a positive learning experience and rate the exercise as valuable; if they do not feel psychological immersion they will experience the learning activity as a failure.* The repeated studies in virtual worlds also confirm Carrie Heeter's discovery that the ratio of people who do not experience immersion is approximately one in four. This means that if educators run a mandatory session in a virtual world for their students, there will always be 25 per cent of students who cannot experience the full effect of the interaction. We may be discovering a brand new form of disability within our classrooms, uncovered by the introduction of this new technology.

Case 8.2 Experiencing disaster management communication in Second Life (with Yung-Fang Chen and El Parker)

Disaster Management and Emergency Planning is a B.Sc. Honours degree taught by Yung-Fang Chen and El Parker at Coventry University within the Department of Geography, Environment and Disaster Management. As part of this degree course, the Islandia exercise was created to provide students with an opportunity to put into practice the theory about how agencies interact and communicate when a disaster takes place. Islandia is a fictional pair of islands in the Pacific Ocean, on which a volcanic eruption has occurred on the northern island and the residents must be evacuated to the southern one. This exercise, although fictional, was based on some real-life scenarios. Students were divided into groups representing various agencies (aid, the military, and so on) to deal with a variety of issues that occurred during the disaster, and, as part of the task, they had to negotiate with each other in order to meet a certain set of goals (unknown to other groups). Before migrating to Second Life this exercise was run in the physical world for several years, with students packed into one big room full of tables representing various agencies' offices. The whole atmosphere during the task was rather chaotic. People struggled to be heard, or even to move between tables, and, frequently, the activity leaked out into other rooms and corridors. The task, however, enthused and engaged the students; an example of practical, problem-based learning at its best.

During the 2009/2010 academic year, this table-top exercise was adapted to run in Second Life. Coventry University has had Second Life presence since 2007, and part of this space was dedicated to developing the environment needed for this activity. The land allocated to the activity was divided into two parts, with a bridge between them, representing the north and the south islands. Buildings for each of the agencies were created and situated within these two areas. Although the number of agencies remained the same, the number of participants was reduced to 14 – two students per group (one being a researcher and the other an information officer). After logging on and finding Coventry Island, students teleported their avatars to the Islandia sim, located their offices and familiarized themselves with the layout of the buildings. During this phase, they had some time to adapt their avatars. The second stage involved initial planning, during which students met with their colleagues in the offices and read through the instructions delivered via notecards on their screen (Figure 8.5). Once the information had been received, the groups had to negotiate a strategy. Then researchers set off to other buildings to interact with information officers from other agencies, who had to stay at their desks at all time (Figure 8.6). Periodically, every researcher had to return to their base to liaise with the information officer. The final phase of the exercise was a debrief conducted in a conference room inworld, so that participants could discuss their experiences of the session (Figure 8.7).

Figure 8.5 **Too many instructions on the screen – reducing immediacy**

Several lessons had been learnt from the earlier activity with Iryna at the University of Warwick (see Case 8.1). One of these lessons was to separate the induction and the actual learning session. Students were given a two-hour session dedicated solely to learning the basics of Second Life, giving them the chance to develop some way-finding abilities. They had 30 minutes just to

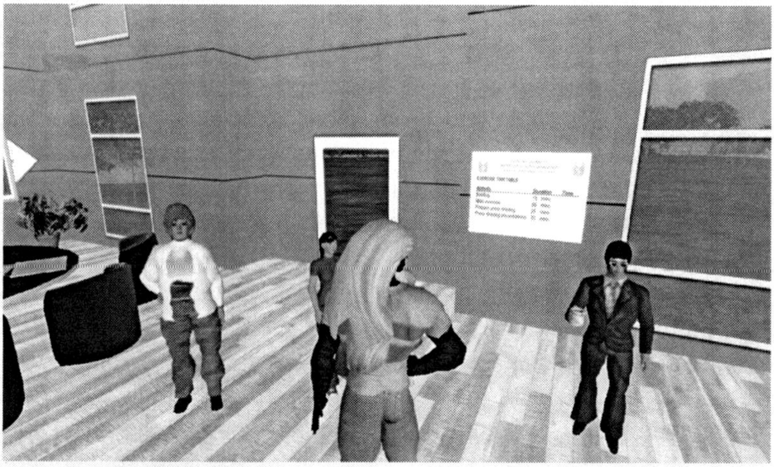

Figure 8.6 **Negotiations at the Northland Government Offices**

Figure 8.7 **Final debrief session in the Community Council Room**

wander around, and by doing so they built up a cognitive map of the buildings hosting the agencies. This resulted in students having no problems with navigation, even though none of them had been in a virtual world before.

Although participants found movement and communication within the platform easy, accessing the notecards through the inworld objects (pieces of paper on the tables in the offices, which were used to add a bit of realism to the exercise) proved more difficult. The problem lay with zooming in the cameras in order to click on the objects. This illustrated how much more complicated manoeuvring is compared to any other forms of locomotion. Once open, students chose to have all the notecards visible on their screen the entire time, so that they could access the instructions easily. There is already a lot of information on-screen in a virtual world, such as the open map windows to help with way-finding, boxes for text chat, as well as the basic interface. Thus, having the instructions on-screen reduced the remaining screen space for the actual viewing of the virtual world, produced 'cognitive overload', and made the entire interaction much less immediate. The suggested solution to this (for any future activities) is to print out the instructions (and perhaps even a map of the space) so that they can be read separately. Even though this reduces the sense of the full integration inworld – and therefore (it could be argued) makes it feel like a less perceptual and psychologically immersive experience – from a practical point of view this approach is much more effective.

The extra time for familiarization may have paid off in other ways too. In contrast to the significant minority who opposed the use of Second Life in Case 8.1, no students disliked it in this exercise (although two of the 14 were ambivalent). However, direct comparisons are difficult. This is partly because of the different subject disciplines, but it is mainly due to the fact that disaster management students were volunteers taking part in a trial, not attending a mandatory session as part of a module. As discussed earlier, there is a significant minority of students who will not engage with learning in a virtual world, and in an optional session these people will normally self-exclude, skewing the results. In contrast to the Warwick case study (Case 8.1), students found the magical forms of locomotion off-putting, with one student stating, 'Sometimes it looked like really a science fiction, because we saw that it's not real, you can fly. It's like a very virtual world.' In addition, the environment created for the task did not induce an emotional resonance for participants. This was mainly because, although it was a disaster management exercise, the content of the environment did not convey any of the signifiers of a catastrophe. One student commented on this lack of emotional involvement:

> I think if you are to be emotionally engaged it would be better to have a real disaster. To take a story from like Haiti or something and put not real names, but real facts, what really happened, you know? Because we didn't really have the feeling to be something real, so we weren't really involved in the disaster. So maybe with people put in there or maybe some collapsed building, or something, you can find the reality.

An alternative mechanism to heighten the emotional engagement was the suggestion by another student of adding a feed, showing a video of a disaster progressing, adding a sense of urgency with updates to the disaster.

The disruptive effect of magical locomotion, and the perceived lack of realism, may have been greater for this exercise because the students were asked to take part in a simulated activity, whereas in Case 8.1 they were only asked to observe (and explore) the spaces. The context for the spaces was therefore very different. However, the fact that this was a simulated activity, requiring role-play and interaction (with a set task and a backstory), had the effect of drawing participants into the space. Despite the reduced immediacy and the absence of elements to actually signify a disaster having taken place, the students' focus on the activity, and their motivation towards using the space to achieve their goal, actually meant that, overall, they were more immersed. For example, when one of the students was asked about the feeling of psychological immersion within the world, the response was:

> I think I was 'in it' because I think the motivation is part of it, so if I wasn't motivated I think I would have been very bored. I think it might help, the motivation, to be 'in' the world. [Interviewer: What was your motivation for?] To be a part of the exercise and know what it's like to be in the field ... because I would like to do that, really, to the future and to have a foot on it.

This was echoed by another student who stated: 'You were really in the game, and you were really concentrating, and you had much to do, which makes it more real.' An explanation of the use of the word 'game' in this context is important. Although it usually indicates that the person is being dismissive about the use of virtual worlds in learning (Kirriemuir, 2010: 3), this is not the case here. In disaster management communication studies, such role-playing exercises are routinely referred to as 'games' and the participants as 'players' (van Haperen, 2001). A third student also remarked on the connection with the space being a result of the activity, saying, 'I was immersed in it 'cause it's like a game, I wanted to complete it.'

Overall, the usefulness of the simulation as a learning exercise was emphasized by all participants, with all of them agreeing with the statement, *I think SL platform exercise has the potential to become one of the methodologies to run crisis exercises and training.* The students' accounts here demonstrate the complexity of the process by which learners experience virtual spaces and their own learning. A common statement about such activities not really being 'in the proper course' is in the context of many students' view that learning is the acquisition of information and does not apply to the practical application and consolidation of those facts. For some learners, reflecting and practising through activities is not learning, meaning that a simulation can only be an adjunct to 'proper learning'. However, as can be seen from the comments above, the value of taking part in such activities is recognized by the students, and helps them 'to have a foot' in their own futures as practitioners.

The experiencing of space, as revealed by the statements above, is only peripherally a function of the technology and exemplifies the distinction between immediacy and immersion. There is little chance of the perception of non-mediation occurring when the view of the space is restricted by an excess of information. Psychological immersion, however, is produced by the motivation of the students to take part in the activity, to practise their learning (though not directly to learn) and to experience, in some form, their role as practitioners. Their desire to change the environment is partly to make it more realistic, partly to reduce the obstructions to immediacy, but mainly to create a more emotionally-charged space, to heighten the emotional experience, and thereby drive forward their sense of being there. It is the resolution to learn (not the resolution on the screen) which adds most to the reality of the virtual space.

Conclusion

The experiences of the students in Cases 8.1 and 8.2 indicate that there is one common fallacy that exists among a variety of hi-tech educational applications – that is, that the key factor in determining a positive experience for learners is the nature of the technology. Although perceptual immersion is inevitably better, with a higher quality rendering on the screen, fewer crashes and reduced lag, these types of consideration are secondary. It is evident from what the participants say that a far greater influence on whether the learning experience is a satisfactory one is the participants' own attitude to a task, as well as the length of time allowed for becoming familiarized with the technology. Usability and immediacy are not deciding factors on whether psychological immersion takes place. It appears that students who become psychologically immersed are compensating for the intrusiveness of the technology, overlooking or incorporating it into their experience. The only two absolute statements that could be made about the immersion of the Warwick students in Case 8.1 are: *no disclosurists felt immersion*, and *all gamers felt immersion*; nothing at all to do with their experience of the technology, and everything to do with their ability (or choice) to engage their belief in the space. The ability of such spaces to promote emotional agency within them helps with such belief; whether this is seeing destruction and dead bodies in a disaster scenario, or the ability to dance on a stage within a theatre. These emotional connections with the inworld elements (Gee's internal signifying systems) and the motivation to engage with the rationale and context for the learning activity (the external system) are what distinguish those who engage belief in the space from those who do not.

In addition, the growing development of psychological immersion can be seen with these experiences. None of the Coventry students in Case 8.2 had problems navigating because they had three times longer to practise. This is an entirely predictable and mundane observation. However, even those Warwick students who had sufficient skills at navigating still could not identify the *feel* of the spaces, whereas the Theatron[3] students (quoted in Chapter 5) could. This extra level of experience requires additional time spent inworld (of the order of months rather than hours) and this is not something we see in other sorts of software use. Immersion develops progressively, from the point when technology occupies the foreground of attention to the point when the user employs it with competency and can then more readily observe the world. To be effective to the highest degree, both activities would have required a longer period of immersion within the environment prior to the subject-specific task. This, however, is not possible within the limited time available on an accredited course. It is this requirement for time with which to learn the platform that, quite reasonably, slows the usage of virtual worlds within education – which is as much of a problem as, for example, limited technological resources. As virtual world activities become more widespread, it may be possible (in the longer term) to ensure that students have a prerequisite learning course in using such spaces. A so-called 'avatar driving licence', which could be acquired as part of the course (suggested by Childs, 2012), could help any prospective educator to have a clearer idea of the learners' inworld abilities and in systematizing the process of learning. It is not possible to ensure that students have acquired the degree of engagement that constitutes inhabiting the spaces. What is feasible, however, is to make certain that they all have the necessary navigation and communication skills required to operate their avatars. This alone would enable lecturers to dedicate all their time in the class to teaching the subject matter, rather than training students in the use of the technology. Furthermore, without the ability to rely on the full psychological immersion of their students, educationalists must select learning activities appropriate to the degree of psychological immersion the class is likely to have formed. However, if those activities require students to become immersed to an extent where they feel situated (not just located) within the world, teachers should not only give them more time inworld but they also need to find ways to help the learner find emotional agency within the space. Like Rosa, they need to keep dancing.

Notes

1. These reports are collected at *http://www.silversprite.com/*.
2. This case study was preliminarily published in the *Proceedings of the International Conference on Education and New Learning Technologies* (EDULEARN09), pp. 1134–45, and in Kuksa and Childs (2010).
3. *http://cms.cch.kcl.ac.uk/theatron/*.
4. The full data are available from Mark Childs's Ph.D. thesis at *http://go.warwick.ac.uk/ep-edrfap* (pp. 180–2).

Part 4
Making sense of space – the practitioner perspective

9

Moving towards the alien 'other' ...

Abstract: This chapter represents the views of practitioners working in virtual worlds on how to make sense of them. It looks into a variety of physical and virtual locations and their applicability to be used for performance practices. It investigates the willingness of the participants to be transformed by such spaces and by the technologies used, and examines the relationships between the viewer and performance and between virtual and physical realities. The authors conclude that nowadays the boundaries between those realities are becoming blurred, with audiences becoming fully incorporated into the performance and with the technology becoming more integrated with them.

Key words: Second Life, Avatar Repertory Theater, translated theatre spaces, novel theatre spaces, translated site-specific spaces, novel site-specific spaces, found spaces.

The very first use of the term *virtual reality* (in 1938 no less) was used, in fact, to describe theatre (Saler, 2012: 204). Both a theatre and a virtual world require a willing suspension of disbelief from a viewer in order for them to feel immersed in the experience. A theatre in a virtual world, therefore, is a 'fourth place' *within* a 'fourth place'. Part 4 brings to the reader the voices of five practitioners who reflect on their understanding of and involvement in virtual worlds as performance spaces. Although representing a range of degrees of experience, and fields of interest, all five embraced the practical side of performance, drama or theatre, and all of them have either created, analysed or acted in virtual spaces. Most have done all of the above. Reviewing and identifying how audiences experience theatre and how different types of virtual performance spaces are constructed, this part attempts to shed some light on the practitioner's relationship to virtual worlds. The following analysis is drawn from interviews and conversations with them, but also from simply observing some of their practical work.

Perspective 1

Sarah Pierpoint: typology for theatrical spaces in the physical world

In 2010, Sarah Pierpoint developed a framework to describe different types of theatrical spaces in the physical world, largely from an audience perspective with the intention of making these explicit for designers. The categories of performance space developed by this process are:

1. the theatre space
2. the found space
3. the site-specific space.

- *The theatre space* represents the many theatre buildings that have been constructed over time, specifically for housing performances. Any type of dedicated theatre space can be placed in this category (for example, theatre-in-the-round, the Globe, a small amateur theatre). There does not need to be a formal seating arrangement for the audience or a positioned stage. If the building has the sole purpose to put on productions that audiences can attend it becomes a theatre space – if there was a school hall that had been designed for that very purpose, then it is a theatre.
- *The found space* is a malleable space that can be changed into a performance space. Unlike the site-specific spaces described below, however, the context of the found space does not relate directly to the performance, so it may not reinforce the audience's experience but also it does not distract from it. Its impact can be, as Robert Smithson says, due to the site being 'a place where a piece should be but isn't' (Kaye, 2000: 91).
- *The site-specific space*, on the other hand, enables another layer to the performance space because it comes with a history of its own, and the audience and performers will respond to this in a different way than a conventional theatre space. In site-specific spaces, the production is adapted to the space, and incorporates elements of the surroundings into its creation. For the space to be used effectively there must be a

dialectic interaction between the setting and the stage. If the disconnect is too great, or at odds with the production, then semiotically the space is effectively a found space. As Andy Field said so succinctly, 'it's not just about finding any old space for new and experimental work regionally, but finding the right kind of space for that work to thrive in' (Field, 2009). The danger with site-specific work is that it can become the main feature for the audience and may overpower the performance.

An audience's perception of theatrical spaces begins to be formulated long before they enter the space. If attending a theatre they may know the building – whether it is big or small, historic or new – and if so they will have already formed an opinion of the space. For popular theatre such as West End musicals the audience will have seen billboards, posters, television adverts and reviews, and may know the story, the songs, the stars and sometimes even the dances before attending the show. Even without this information they will know to some extent what to expect from the space: a fixed stage, perhaps with curtains, in parallel to the audience who are sitting in small, uncomfortable seats with a lack of legroom. Other elements of the experience will be familiar too: the bother of moving to let people sit down and get up, the interval, the momentary silence as the show begins, and the applause at the end. These conventions are reassuring and they are all part of the show. Gay McAuley describes the spectator's relationship with space in theatre as the fictional part of the social event. At times, the audience will be more focused on interacting with the people around them in the space than on the performance itself. A spectator may have to turn around and ask someone to be quiet, or, as McAuley suggests, male and female spectators may admire someone in the auditorium (McAuley, 2000: 265).

Away from conventional theatrical spaces, however, audiences do not know the rules or conventions, and it may be that they will remain oblivious even after the performance has taken place. A found space does not inform the audience of any social conventions or history; it is possibly completely unknown. If the performance is set in a site-specific space, such as a castle, the audience possibly will know its history and its purpose. However, for both types of performance spaces, audience members will have much less, or no, idea of what they will experience than they would in a theatre space because all of the signifiers of the usual performance location, with which they are familiar, are absent. This may alienate some members of the audience, and in order to overcome this many productions choose to provide some level of instruction or guidance to the audience so that they will have some idea of what to expect. But, conversely, this is likely to entice some viewers, since they may feel more comfortable outside of a conventional theatre building or intrigued by something out of the ordinary.

How these different spaces can influence the perceptions of the audiences can be analysed according to a series of factors which distinguish the forms of engagement with each type of space; this framework identifies the following elements:

- The past, present and future of the space.
- The research that is required in order to use the space effectively.
- How text needs to be adapted to the constraints and affordances of the space.
- The colour and composition of design enabled and constrained by the space.
- The impact the space has on the embodiment experienced by the performer.
- The role of the spectator within the performance.
- The audience's preconceptions about the space.

The taxonomy described above was used as a model for developing a similar description for virtual theatre spaces. Through the same grounded approach of looking at a range of theatres, identifying their separate aspects and grouping these into discrete categories with the minimum of redundancy and overlap, a series of categories was identified (Childs and Pierpoint, 2010). This taxonomy is developed further below, with, firstly, a range of testimonies from experienced theatre practitioners who have worked extensively in virtual worlds.

Perspective 2

Gameela Wright: producing theatre in a virtual world

AvaJean Westland is the name of Gameela's avatar. Gameela is an actor and producer with a theatre group based in Second Life called the Avatar Repertory Theater (ART). What follows are descriptions of her work.

'I think that virtual space lends itself to more imagination, more choices and more challenges. One has to think in four dimensions and one isn't hindered by real-life limitations such as gravity. But because of this, you have a tougher audience to satisfy; virtual world occupants. There are so many avenues open to us in virtual worlds; the only cost is time and labour.

Our work in ART is mostly determined by either the subject matter or our audience. We have performed in builds that were simulations of real-world environments. In those cases, we were commissioned to perform there and so our work was directly led by those commissioning us. For example, we performed Shakespeare at the San Diego Pavilion sim as it is done in real life.

Since Second Life is relatively young, the theatre-going audience doesn't really have expectations based on the location. Places come and go, change their look and structure all the time. The exception is if there is a "theme" as there is on many role-playing sims. If you're doing classical theatre, people will expect that look and feel, but not necessarily demand it. Virtual world audiences are open to change and alteration. In terms of freedom of expression, within the constraints of good taste, or if the space is defined by a theme, the sky is the limit.

I think everyone has a learning curve in terms of adjusting to the virtual world, but it is a quick one. Once you learn how to operate the tools provided (for example being able to move the camera viewpoint independently of the avatar) it doesn't take long to be comfortable in their use. This still means, however, that although an advanced Second Life member will know how to move their camera around, a newer member may not.

One of the major goals of *Alice in WonderSLand* (Figure 9.1) was to bring the audience into the experience. Personally, I don't see the point of always sitting in a theatre seat and watching the action on stage when there are so many other things we can do in a virtual world. When our audience actually fell down the rabbit hole with Alice they were absolutely thrilled, every single performance.

Figure 9.1 ***Alice in WonderSLand*** **performance by ART in Second Life**

Source: image reproduced with permission of ART

In a traditional theatre set-up, the preconception is that the audience is going to just sit there and watch a performance. This in itself is limiting. In a virtual theatre, the audience is expected to behave as they would in real life with one exception: they are given a bit more leeway when "talking" via text during a performance. Since they are instructed to keep their microphones off (just as people are asked not to speak during a performance in real theatre) there is no way to know if they are enjoying the performance or how so. So, many will run gestures that show up as text and sound for applause or they will make a whimsical comment at something they've seen or heard. This is gratifying to the actors and production staff. The actual design of the space, as it was in *Alice*, lends itself to having the audience be immersed in the performance and to comment on it. The audience is always informed about what they can and cannot do, and what they need to do to ensure that the experience is positive for all, so they are asked to remove highly-scripted items, not to speak in voice, and to cover their avatars (some people had their real-life children watching the show) so as to not offend anyone. Lastly, if anyone distracts the audience and causes a problem, they are promptly ejected from the sim.

In virtual theatre, the voice is the most important part of the performance since we have limits on what we can do technologically to evoke emotion or mood. The size or layout of the space has no bearing on vocal quality as there is no need to "project" one's voice unless the scene calls for it specifically. In general, the space either can be just that – a space – or it can become a character in itself – lending the actor and the audience a better context of the story. But it is there to support the actor, not the other way around. There can be, however, restrictions in movement, just as there are in real life. "Blocking" a scene is as necessary in Second Life as it is in a real-world theatre, perhaps even more so, since movement can give the audience information as to what is going on.

The piece can be influenced by the space and vice versa. In the case of *Alice*, we tricked the audience to some extent. Though they were in a 360 degree space they were seated slightly away from the sets and the actors. So when it came time for Alice to fall down the hole and to swim in her own tears, the audience was happily surprised that suddenly their avatars were doing the same. Again, in a virtual world, we are limited only by our imaginations and technical resources.'

Perspective 3

Ian Upton: creating experiences for audiences in virtual spaces

Ian Upton is an artist and designer working predominantly in Second Life. Below are his views on how to emotionally engage audiences with a virtual space. He talks about the creation of a piece called *Ritual Circle*, which was created on the (public) mainland of Second Life (Figure 9.2).

'My main experience is in setting up events, spaces, installations, but not in traditional theatre. People enter my performing spaces for an experience, rather than to observe a piece they're not part of. What is interesting about the development of my practice in virtual environments is that I started off by emulating a real-world

Figure 9.2 ***Ritual Circle***

Source: image reproduced with permission of Ian Upton

model. Once you free yourself from being limited by the constraints of the physical world, it actually all becomes very obvious. For example, a real-world model is to set up a theatre space and then move the scenery into that space; whereas in a virtual environment it is actually easier to move the spectators. In addition, the line between the audience and the performers is totally blurred. In Second Life it is completely normal to be asked to wear an outfit for a performance, so you actually become part of the set. For example, in *The Tempest* the audience sat on barrels and were dressed in costumes that matched the stylistic theme of the production.

In the physical world, places like a church or an ancient stone circle have a history, which in itself produces a certain emotional response in the audience. Thus, one of the things I try to do is to create virtual spaces that have that same resonance. There is a question as to whether this is possible, however; whether you can create a virtual space that has some sort of gravitas in its own right, and has presence. How do you create a virtual space that possesses that sort of quality, where you can just go and be, and where this 'go-and-be-ingness' is somehow amplified or held in there? What aspects do you deal with inworld that start to tap into those kind of elements?

The nearest I got was a stone circle (in Second Life). In order to design it, people were sending me drawings over a period of time, which I applied to the textures of the standing stones. Two things started to happen as a consequence. For people who were participants in the stone circle experience, they were actually leaving a little bit of themselves in that space, not only artefacts but also their memories. But even when people who knew nothing about it came into the space, they started to get this feeling that things had happened there. Although this wasn't a replica of any stone circle that exists in the physical world, the circle had started to accrue and gain its own history. The shape is basically still there, but the stone circle itself is gone, and a number of people actually felt a loss when it went. These feelings were not simply about its aesthetic appeal, but most referred to the circle as a space with which they made an emotional connection.

A necessary part of that experience was the journey into the space of the stone circle and actually stepping into it. There wasn't an entrance as such. You had to walk through a forest hollow like a crater filled with trees with the circle in a little clearing at the bottom. You rezzed into the dense forest and walked down and the space just opened up. This design is important when places are constructed on the mainland of Second Life, as opposed to on islands, because other things impede. I streamed sound to the space, which I find makes a big difference. When you meet up with others at the beginning of the path and then step into the space together, the magical psychological transformation happens and stays with you while you are inside the space.

What is interesting is that, perhaps because I work in Second Life eight hours a day, when I log in I don't feel that this is the act of transition, this is just an extension of me. However, when my avatar goes into those spaces, there is quite a strong difference, and I would argue that a lot of the people I know quite well (and they are all people who have been using Second Life for a long time) would probably say something similar. There isn't that "I'm stepping into the avatar" experience. It's more that the avatar is just a little bit extra to me, and this is the avatar who is going to step in.

The direction my work is going in is ultimately about getting rid of the technology. One of the things I am quite keen to try is where you blur the technologies, and use 3D stereo for creating almost a traditional theatre space, in which the virtual imposes and vice versa. It is sort of 'de-technologizing' that space, in order to reach the stage when your experience is just an extension of yourself. Often new technologies when they emerge, they're not quite there, and you are always explaining what the problem is – whether that is in context or ability. But when the technology becomes obvious, you just don't notice it.'

Perspective 4

Joff Chafer: site-specificity of virtual worlds

Joff Chafer is an actor and academic based at Coventry University. He has worked for many years in both physical and virtual performances. Below is his interpretation of defining the role of virtual worlds. He talks about different theatre production companies involved in creating performances for immersive virtual environments, and about the ways in which they managed to influence conventional staging techniques and performative practices.

'The original reason I was in Second Life was to look for a site-specific performance space. For the most part with ART we work with complete blank spaces to start with, which could be a whole sim. The joy of that is that for something like *The Tempest*, for example, you can build the island (on which the performance took place), the ship and other things (Figure 9.3). The performance of *The Tempest* made a full use of the surrounding area – so we had

Figure 9.3 **ART's *The Tempest* in Second Life**

Source: image reproduced with permission of Joff Chafer

the audiences floating on boxes while watching the show. However, the space *per se* is not completely blank, and the site is not completely irrelevant to the performance. The space we performed in was Second Life, and Second Life has its own unique characteristics, features and also limitations. The possibilities it does present mean that almost anything can happen. In a sense, it is a site-specific performance, with Second Life itself (not a building *in* Second Life) being that site. In addition, you're playing for a specific community there, one of many sub-communities in Second Life, but it's that community that is your audience.

Some other theatre companies, for example Second Front, do "happenings", where they will go to a random space within Second Life (for example a shopping mall) to perform. This approach is much more pertinent to the idea of "you have got a space, how does that affect what you're doing". I think from the ART point of view it is completely different; the space we're using is Second Life, not a shopping mall in Second Life.

Translating from other spaces is just bringing existing things from one environment into another, rather than creating something new or working with what is available. For example, *Metropolis* is a Second Life recreation of a film that has a very specific design aesthetic going for it. This performance was predominantly design led, with excellent technical elements, but the acting seemed like an add-on and didn't really make a great deal of difference. It was more about building some fantastic thing, and doing brilliant camerawork and clever technical tricks, rather than being drawn to playing a character to understand their motivation.

With the Metaverse Shakespeare Company (MSC) having their performances in a recreation of the Globe there is a sense that they are acting in a space that has some sort of history – even though it is just a copy and can never be the original. However, this virtual theatre has been around for a few years now, and it is starting to get its own history. The Globe is an excellent build aesthetically and it adds to an appreciation of theatre in Second Life simply by being there. But its reason to exist is because it is a recreation of a historical artefact, with the performances staged there being an added bonus. There's another Globe theatre on Renaissance Island which isn't as good aesthetically, but it is situated in a living environment so it has more of an emotional resonance. If you are going to the MSC Globe you are going there to see the theatre, whereas on Renaissance Island you would be looking at other different things happening there. However, if someone decides to produce a performance on Renaissance Island they would immediately have two advantages:

1. there is a community already in place there, so there is an audience on hand; and
2. you will be working with something that is not an imposing structure, which frees you to do more.

The Globe itself is site-specific, but at times it is not. It was designed to recreate an existing space with a sense of what the history of it might be, but I'm not sure it really affects the performances so much. When you wheel on a huge great set, it's not really site-specific. It's a stage; it doesn't really matter where it is (from the point of view of how the play is constructed). But it might make a difference for the audience in the sense that, for them, this is an important event they are going to, regardless of whether it is in the real Globe or in one of the virtual Globes.

> The unique thing about ART is that every theatrical space gets packed up and boxed away in case it needs to come out again. It is different for the Globe – it will only last as long as the owners can afford to sustain it. There is an exception, however, even for ART, and that is the space in which we do the Friday night gigs, the Greek Archon theatre, which was originally used for Greek tragedies but is now used for anything. Like the Globe on Renaissance Island, it has a community linked to it but no history associated with the space itself. History in Second Life is a community history – not a design or space history. Second Life is primarily a 3D social networking site, and people within it have formed communities and are subverting the space for their own ends, whether they are going to dance clubs, playing role-play games, creating galleries or doing theatre. Fundamentally, if the communities weren't there it would be irrelevant whether a building was there or not; whereas in the real world the buildings don't need the people to exist, they would still be there and have their own meanings and history.'

Reflecting on the above perspectives and developing a conceptual framework for performance spaces in the virtual worlds

The idea of virtual performance is somewhat problematic for many people. Peter Brook's famous quote on the essence of theatre is that 'I can take any empty space and call it a bare stage. A man walks across this empty space whilst someone else is watching him, and this is all that is needed for an act of theatre to be engaged' (Brook, 1968: 9). The point of Brook's statement is that this is the bare minimum that could count as performance. In a virtual world no one is physically present, and performance is conveyed via the movement of avatars and sometimes voice (or more commonly text) – so what does this mean for an act of theatre to be engaged? If it is accepted as a performance, then what if the avatars are partly operated by an artificial agent, or even wholly (but imperceptibly) replaced by an agent? At what point does that cease to be a performance? Some practitioners would state that virtual performance is self-contradictory, and that one must be physically co-present for it to count as performance, yet there are numerous groups operating in virtual worlds that define themselves as theatrical performers. The accounts of the practitioners above demonstrate the extent to which the spaces in virtual worlds are very much real to those who act and design within them. There is also no doubt that the way in which digital and physical spaces are performed is quite different. This difference, however, is no greater than when theatre practice alters from one physical site to another. The same considerations take place about the venue, about the communities approached, about generating interest, and about meeting the requirements of the space. Indeed, the performances that make use of the specific affordances of virtual worlds and appeal to the communities within those spaces are site-specific. Very often, however, the sites used for the act of theatre inworld (as Joff argued) are not pre-existing, re-purposed spaces; they are created specifically for each performance.

Another line of the above argument included the distinction between site-specific spaces that have been translated inworld from other media, such as *Metropolis* (a recreation of Fritz Lang's film). Although adopting non-theatrical spaces is a good example of how creators develop complex sets and scripted objects and control camera viewpoints – providing visually stunning experiences for their audiences – such spaces are not primarily created as platforms for performance. For example, translated theatre spaces created for a variety of purposes, such as multiple Globe theatres, the Theatre of Epidavros (one of the Theatron[3] Project's reconstructions) and the Birmingham Hippodrome (created by Daden Ltd for the Birmingham Royal Ballet), are most concerned with design of the buildings. Of course, the history of these spaces within the virtual world is informed by their history in the physical world. Therefore, their value is in the capacity for making use of that past knowledge through translating it to the digital medium. On the other hand, the novel theatre sites in Second Life are a category of space that is still recognizably theatrical (with a stage and auditorium), but is not translated from the physical world. These are often home to performances but exist primarily as a role-play place for the community. For example, the Caledon Gaiety Theatre (discussed in the previous chapter) is a music hall venue with a Steampunk aesthetic; the Karnak Stage exists within an Ancient Egyptian role-play area; and the Hatchie Haven auditorium is part of the Isle of Wyrms's role-play sim, where baby dragons (known as hatchies) and other small forms of avatars known as tinies can put on performances. The Renaissance Island Globe Theatre belongs more in this category, mainly because its historical accuracy is of less importance to its designers than its role within the Renaissance community of which it is part.

The performing spaces described above are still recognizably traditional forms of theatre, although adapted to the contexts in which they are placed (for example, small seats for the diminutive hatchies, or pseudo-Victorian embellishments in the Steampunk scenario). The typology of spaces therefore becomes a 2 × 2 matrix as shown in Figure 9.4.

Translated theatre spaces	**Novel theatre spaces**
Examples: The MSC Globe Theatre, Birmingham Hippodrome, Theatre of Epidavros.	Examples: The Caledon Gaiety Theatre, Karnak, Hatchie Haven, The Renaissance Island Globe Theatre.
Translated site-specific spaces	**Novel site-specific spaces**
Examples: *Metropolis*, *The Wall*.	Examples: *Alice in WonderSLand*, *Ritual Circle*, *The Tempest*.

Figure 9.4 Typology of theatre space in virtual worlds

The most innovative of theatrical experiences, however, are those that push the definitions of virtual performance in ways that begin to exploit the new affordances of virtual worlds; those that fall into the novel quasi-site-specific spaces, and are not translated from other media nor from the physical world; and those that do not appropriate any of the conventional structures of theatrical spaces. It is these spaces that have hosted the work of the remaining practitioner in this chapter. These performances challenged viewers' preconceptions, and reinvented social conventions and audience–performer relationships. The main goal of the *Extract/Insert* performance and installation, which took place at the Herbert Art Gallery and Museum in Coventry in October–November 2012, was to break away from the separate categories of physical and virtual. This was a collaboration between Ian Upton and Joff Chafer with Stelarc, whose work was introduced briefly in Chapter 1.

Extract/Insert was comprised of two spaces (real and virtual) with a large screen in between (onto which a scene from Second Life was stereoscopically projected). There was also a raised platform, on which people could stand and be projected onto a virtual screen in Second Life, a smaller separate screen at the back of the room (for individual avatars to be visualized), and a series of cameras. Anyone passing through the gallery would hear the sounds of the virtual world and be welcomed in by two ushers, who would explain the technology and anticipated experience to them. Then the participants were given a pair of polarized glasses that converted the stereoscopic projection of the virtual world and the life-size avatars into 3D. In the corresponding virtual space, participants who entered the Second Life *Extract/Insert* room could also see images of real people in the gallery, projected to scale with their avatars. For some participants (approximately one in three), viewing this installation was a bewildering and alienating experience. For the majority, however, it was an astounding transition out of the normal notion of reality into something transformative. People would return repeatedly, acknowledging the avatars they met, recognizing them on sight. Within the virtual world, participating avatars would stay for most of the opening hours of the virtual gallery (and since most were US-based, this was often very late at night or early in the morning because of the time-zone differences) and interact with the physical world, perform dance routines and answer questions. Perhaps the most engaging experience was to high-five an avatar – albeit only visually (with the help of the 3D projection) and with no tactile impression. Some of the most involved real-world participants posed for photographs, standing next to the screen at the edge of spaces – avatar and physical body to scale alongside each other. This installation created the illusion of a window into the other reality, not only blurring the division between the real and the virtual but also *mingling* them (see Figures 9.5 and 9.6).

Figure 9.5 ***Extract/Insert*** **installation**

Source: image reproduced with permission of Dena de Rougemont

Figure 9.6 **The view of the physical space from the Second Life *Extract/Insert* installation**

Source: image reproduced with permission of JoJa Dhara

Perspective 5

Stelarc: Extract/Insert *and the future of humanity*

'The idea of *Extract/Insert* is to mesh the actual space with a virtual space (in this case Second Life). A person visiting the Herbert Gallery can be extracted from the physical room and inserted into Second Life, while simultaneously avatars visiting inworld might be extracted and inserted into the gallery itself. It's the idea of having an interface between the actual and the virtual and being able to interact seamlessly between the two. Because the experience is in 3D, it optically merges the two worlds together more adequately.

For me, there's always been an interest in this idea of performing with mixed realities. Underlying this interest is the notion that we're no longer merely biological bodies, our lives are accelerated by our machines, our instruments provide us a greater and extended sensory perception and we have to manage data streams in virtual systems. This leads us as humans to actually be a kind of chimera of meat, metal and code. This means that we have to increasingly devise better strategies for seamlessly switching between the biological, the mechanical and the virtual. And of course now with augmented reality, we are doing that on a daily basis. It is this seamless switching that we are trying to convey through this installation.

Extract/Insert is both a sensory and aesthetic experience, but it is also a technically interesting one as well. Of course what people take away from a work of art is open to interpretation, and it wouldn't be an artwork if there wasn't a certain ambivalence and uncertainty. We are not doing journalism, we are not trying to be explicit, but what is implicit is this meshing of the virtual and the actual. There is also, further to that, a speculation on that meshing; that perhaps what's important is not real life (or Second Life), but a third life where eventually autonomous and intelligent avatars might want to access a surrogate body and perform with it in the real world. So then there won't be this kind of master–slave set-up, where you are sitting at a computer physically controlling your avatar in Second Life, but, rather, an avatar might want to access your body and operate with it in the real world.

What all of this technology generates is alternative operational possibilities, and also it questions what it means to be human and what it means to be alive. With our robots and our artificial agents we have to come up with vocabularies of behaviour that maintain our sense of "aliveness" in these environments and generate new forms of it. So technology isn't simplistically about information but also about haptic manifestations, sustaining touch, emotion and affect, which is a complex process to be navigated.

All three of us have performed in Second Life. The interest for me was initially exploring the performative possibilities in a virtual world, where gravity need not exist, where you could perform with a virtual body that could fly and float, and be animated in unexpected ways. I wanted to explore how you could map sounds to objects and interact with them and perform with them, so you compose the sounds by choreographing the movements of your body. With a Kinect sensor, what was interesting was that you were able to stand in front of the screen and without resorting to the arrow keys on a keyboard or a mouse but instead by using gestures and by tilting your body backwards and forwards and twisting left or right, you could activate your avatar, enabling you to navigate through Second Life simply via your body movements and your arm gestures. In performances, for example at the Warhol Museum in Pittsburgh and at the Tate Modern, we had a repertoire of gestures, so, for example, the right side generated the

navigation of the avatar through Second Life, and the left side of my body triggered particular animations, which generated sounds. Thus, with that combination of left and right arm gestures I could create some very interesting performative possibilities and make that physical and virtual connection more apparent for a real-life audience.

McLuhan had a very interesting definition of technology – that it is the external organ of the body (1964: 41–7). So we have evolved as a soft body with these soft internal organs, in order to function in a natural world, but also in an increasingly complex technological terrain. What is happening now is that we are engineering additional external organs – in other words our technologies, our instruments, our machines and our computers – to enable the body to amplify its physical possibilities. What it means to be human is therefore perhaps not remaining human at all. We have always been constantly changing; we have always been generating new information and images which force us to re-evaluate what the world is and how we operate as bodies. And those bodies have always been augmented and extended in different ways. So I think it is not meaningful to imagine that there is an intrinsic human and that we are somehow going towards an alien "other". What it means to be human, in fact, is to become that alien other.'

Conclusion

From the accounts of practitioners working in virtual worlds it appears that the range of ways in which people make sense of spaces, and in which performances take place, is far more complex than the corresponding sense-making in the real world. As Sarah Pierpoint notes in her typology of spaces above (see p. 122), physical locations have their own history, their own surroundings and their own relationship to the semiotics of theatre, any of which may or may not be applicable to the performance. In addition, the audiences will also have their own preconceptions and knowledge of conventions of different spaces. In virtual worlds, however, theatres may be translated from the physical world, in which case they can carry across their historical perspective, or they may accrue new histories inworld. They may be located within a community, or they may stand alone without any context. Those created specifically for a performance may be ephemeral, but the community that attends them is more likely to be permanent. The *raison d'être* for the performance itself may also vary. For a translated setting it may be only a secondary activity, or just an opportunity to showcase the design.

The relationship between audiences and the spaces is also more fragmented in the virtual world, not only by the audiences' knowledge of the piece but also by their sophistication with respect to the conventions of the specific type of theatre. In the physical world, audiences need to be informed about the structure of site-specific and found spaces, but, as Gameela notes, they also need to be made aware of technicalities such as voice and the movement of their camera, in order to not just make sense of the show and know how to behave but also simply to *view* the performance (see p. 125 above). A space that depends on audience members' camming (that is, moving their camera positions to gain a better perspective) will be viewed differently by an experienced person to an inexperienced one. As Joff Chafer explains in a supplement to his contribution to this chapter:

> One thing that permanently worries me is what the audience sees and whether and how much we rely on the audience being able to use their cameras. When blocking, you ignore the audience, but coming from a real-world acting background there are dos and don'ts. For example you never turn your back on the audience, you always make sure that they can see, you're not blocking other people, you're not upstaging. I know there will be plenty of people there who are camming around to make it look good for them, but there will always be the people there who have only just gone in and are just sitting there and going 'Oh what's this on my screen?' and not 'Now what's going on?'

In the physical world there may be impediments to viewing the stage, but we can usually assume people know how to look in the right direction. The relationship between audience and performance can also be blurred with audiences being fully incorporated into the performance, as Gameela, Ian and Joff all note. In her discussion above on the role of the spectator in the physical world, Sarah Pierpoint describes a similar alteration in relationship: the spectators sitting passively in a traditional space can become 'spectagonists' in found and site-specific spaces; they can be located in the performance space, and incorporated into the action. This blurring of spectator and performer therefore has its precedent in the physical, but reaches new heights of integration in the virtual.

The idea of virtual worlds, ritual spaces and theatres as fourth places, which require belief and which exercise a transformation on those who participate, is challenged by Ian Upton. He finds the ritual and theatrical spaces more transformative than the virtual world, as the virtual world is simply an extension of his natural being. This echoes Stelarc's exploration of technology as permanently transformative, rather than something one puts on and takes off. What emerges from this discussion is that not only are our new experiences of spaces dependent on how our associations, preconceptions and previous experiences of those spaces intersect with their design, their purpose and the creators' understanding of us as participants, but that those experiences also depend on our willingness to be transformed by the space. When those spaces are located within a technological environment, the degree to which we make sense of them is also determined by our willingness to be transformed by that technology. For example, do we feel our avatar to be an extension of ourselves or, following the precedent of Stelarc, are we willing to become physically connected to that avatar? As the boundary between virtual and physical realities becomes blurred, or even as those realities become mingled (as in the mixed reality setting of *Extract/Insert*), the technology may come to be more seamless and more invisible, but in so doing it becomes more integrated with us. Experiencing spaces does not then simply depend on us being transformed while we inhabit them – it also requires us to embrace the movement towards the alien 'other' and take that transformation permanently into ourselves.

Part 5
Conclusion

10

The future of spaces – physical or virtual?

Abstract: The concluding chapter of this book revisits such an important issue as immersiveness and how it influences the way we communicate and interact with and within virtual worlds. It looks into how physical spaces translate into digital and virtual spaces, impacting on our emotions, learning and creativity. Here, the authors define what space actually means in the context of their work, emphasizing the importance of its design, accessibility, sustainability, and the intentions of its producers. They discuss the collision of virtual and physical worlds, which creates a new synthesis but also raises the question of who is responsible for managing digital footprints. The chapter concludes with the coining of a new term – 'phyrtual' – which describes a new type of reality we are facing, where our physical bodies are constantly extended throughout the virtual.

Key words: space, manipulability, reciprocation, responsiveness, immersion, 'phyrtual'.

New media continuously and irreversibly changed human perceptions of spaces we inhabit. The title of this book, *Making Sense of Space*, prompts us to define what *space* actually means in the context of our work. The concept of a three-dimensional volume with orthogonal axes may work for a mathematical or physical model, but sense-making implies that for us to understand something *as* a space is a matter of how its semiotic content appeals to our imagination and ways of perceiving the world. Throughout the book we have discussed physical spaces and how they translate into digital and virtual spaces; we have examined how virtual worlds (and the spaces within them) influence our emotions, ways of communicating to one another, and our ability to be creative. The question posed in the introduction section of the book was whether digital media platforms are able to constitute *locations* and whether interactivity is key in order for us to feel immersed (psychologically) while exploring virtual worlds. One in four participants in such experiences (particularly in learning activities) would probably say 'No'. For them, these spaces will always remain simply images appearing on the screen and not 'virtually' real. The rest, however, will experience the full or partial emotional effect of the interaction with them. The concern was voiced as to whether this inability to connect with virtual worlds and the spaces within them is a new form of disability. Or could it be that those users simply cannot break through the technology barrier? Although such findings should be considered carefully when planning any mandatory learning session or activity in such environments, much research is still needed in order to understand from where resistance, or inability, to fully experience virtuality arises. For example, the prejudice against technology and its 'immateriality' still exists, not only among educationalists and students but also among creative practitioners. In this book, we have attempted to present examples of the breaking of the boundaries between the physical and the virtual, 'mingling' these two realities together and having an impact on the audience perception of what these different realities can contribute to artistic practice. In recent years, we have witnessed an acceleration of interest in the generation of digital cultural heritage spaces. Some researchers criticize this trend, observing that the current practice of the majority of cultural institutions to embrace virtual presence by reconstructing their existing buildings in 3D and digitizing their collections is problematic. Undoubtedly, such developments led to some great projects and networks being established, helped visitors to get access to the base of knowledge remotely, and assisted researchers in analysing historical artefacts. However, there is an issue as to how sustainable these new virtual cultural sites are. Although virtual, these spaces still need to be maintained. Currently, even the most sophisticated digital worlds cannot self-update. This might happen in the future with the emergence of the intelligent agents promised by Web 4.0 technologies, but, to date, digital sustainability is still an issue. Furthermore, any space also needs to be found, by, for example, signposting in the real world, or by creating comprehensive, consistent and compatible paradata in the virtual world. Initiatives such as the London Charter propose a set of principles to enable the best possible execution and implementation of 3D sites and objects, which will help with ensuring their sustainable long-term existence and accessibility. Finally, the design of digital spaces (and associated devices) is crucial in order to communicate the intentions of their producers clearly to the end-users, and should include semantic information about the environments, making them more interactive and, in fact, more attractive to engage with.

Virtual worlds have been employed to accommodate a wide variety of human day-to-day behaviour, and, as a consequence, are now firmly integrated into our daily lives. Although from a business perspective new media platforms are loci from which to deliver more value-added services, more ways to sell products and better methods to ensure the continuity of the relationship with contemporary users, we, as consumers, are no longer satisfied just with being observers of these spaces. It is no longer sufficient. We want to partake, interact and even contribute to the development cycle of an application or a product, to an art installation or a performance, to our learning and communication. The future of virtual worlds requires that providers and creators, whether business- or art-orientated, are fully aware of the personal and involved interrelationship that people have with the virtual spaces in which they live. This bring us back to the question of whether virtual spaces are actually *locations*, and we will break down this discussion into sections below, in order to arrive at a possible answer.

Digital to virtual: is cyberspace a space?

Jon Ippolito argues that cyberspace (as a spatial metaphor) is a practical necessity determined by the unpreparedness of our culture to the steep technological learning curve we experienced in the 1990s (Ippolito, 1999). William Gibson, and his 1984 novel *Neuromancer*, was responsible for prominently embedding the concept of cyberspace in our minds and our society. This was something 'our culture had prepared everyone to understand: a chase sequence through an imagined space' (Ippolito, 1999: 16–17). Indeed, cyberspace is a common metaphor and yet its usefulness has been challenged, for example by Katherine Olson more than a decade ago (Olson, 2000). While acknowledging that using such figures of speech in accommodating new technologies is natural, and noting that early expressions drew on parallels to communications networks (ibid.: 10), nevertheless she argues that there is a tendency to employ spatial metaphors (such as web*sites*, for example) more widely and less usefully than is appropriate. On a legal level, she emphasizes, the idea of the Internet as a space has led to the concept of cybertrespass, meaning that the unwanted communication violates one's space rather than one's things (ibid.: 14). In addition, it has led to the idea that the information that exists on one's display is a separate place from the location where that display sits and, therefore, subject to different laws than those that apply to the actual physical setting.

However, when we move from the realm of computer networks to 3D worlds of virtual reality (the second branch of cyberspace) the idea that this is a purely metaphorical use of the word *space* is not so obvious. Unlike the separate web pages of a website, the space in a virtual world has three dimensions, which can be navigated and moved through with changing perspectives in a manner very similar to the physical world. We have a reality in that space through the presence of our avatars, who give us the ability to interact with objects and other people inworld, constituting a strong sense of location. In fact, it is that self-presence in a virtual world that can make a MUD feel more like a space than a 3D model. Evidently, a 3D reconstruction of an artefact or a cultural heritage site is more perceptually immersive than a purely text-based MUD, but it still does not bestow on us a reality within it due to the disembodied way we interact with it. Rebecca Bryant states that similar to physical space, cyberspace comprises at least four sub-concepts: place (where?), distance (how far?), size (how big?) and route (navigation) (Bryant, 2001). This definition is hardly the new post-geographical insight that some of us were hoping for. One might call VR self-contradictory (Olson, 2000: 14), which, in fact, it is. 'Virtual' originates from the Latin word *vertus*, translating as *truth*, but corresponds better to something being more *truth-like*, which, in its turn, could be interpreted as *unreal*. Michele Ryan explored the etymology of the phrase 'virtual reality' and concluded that it is a fake reality, one which is not real, or make-believe. An opposing viewpoint is that we can invest whatever importance we choose to in alternative realities, that a space in which we move, interact, have friendships and communities may not be completely solid and independently real, but it is *virtually* reality (Ryan and Childs, 2011: 256–7). It is the significance we give to the objects, people and societies in our *virtually real* surroundings, and the very fact that they feel like such, that enables us to have emotional agency within virtual spaces. It is because these spaces require our intention to engage belief in them, in order to make them real to us, and in order to make virtual worlds space-like. Therefore, the space that we inhabit in a virtual world is not habitable because it is a space; it is a space because we inhabit it. It is up to us to choose what we want the cyberspace to be.

Moving from physical to virtual: losses and gains

In 1998, Max Velmans posed the following set of questions about three types of realities – physical, psychological and virtual:

> In our predominantly materialist culture we take it for granted that the physical world is real. But in what sense are experiences, thoughts and feelings real? And what about virtual realities? Are they physical, psychological, or somewhere in between?
>
> (Velmans, 1998: 45)

Velmans argues that with the use of the appropriate (physical) devices and through the information they provide, the user obtains an impression that virtual worlds extend into the physical world. But, in truth, such worlds have no actual 3D physical extension, and their very existence fully depends on the information delivered by the physical equipment. So, what does it mean to move from the physical reality into the virtual one? Willing suspension of disbelief (or engagement of belief)? Virtualization associated with technology? Or is there no need for such a move at all, because (as VR conjecture theory states) 'this world is a virtual reality created by processing, not an objective reality that exists inherently by itself alone' (Whitworth, 2010: 227)?

These questions can be answered by, firstly, looking at the technology and how it influences our senses. In the introduction to this book we discussed the factors that contribute to making technologies immersive, which are a combination of their realness or vividness. Vividness is a term employed by Jonathan Steuer in 1995, which he defined as comprised of *the breadth of the technology* (the range of senses it engages) and its *depth* (technical attributes such as resolution) (Steuer, 1995). By breadth of technology, Steuer referred not only to visual tools for conveying virtual or remote spaces, but also auditory, taste-smell and haptic (force-feedback or touch) systems, as well as a means to orientate the body within those spaces (ibid.: 41–3). Depth of technology refers to a better resolution, higher refresh rates and stereo sound. Breadth and depth both make perceptual immersion greater. Interactivity too is a prominent contributor to a sense of immersion through the actions of:

- *Manipulability*: the extent to which a participant can change the environment. The more things we can manipulate (range) and the degree to which we can alter them (fineness) add to the sense of realism.

- *Reciprocation*: the amount of feedback from the digital space about the changes we have made, whether from objects or other users within the environment.
- *Responsiveness*: refers to the speed of the feedback, rather than the degree to which it takes place, and so is different from reciprocation.

These are factors that we take for granted in the real world but which can be lost when one moves from the physical to the virtual. The physical has complete immersiveness, though visual impairments may disrupt this. The physical world supports the entire range of senses; there are touch interfaces (skin), sound, high resolution and no lag. Mobility is more of an issue. Walking and manoeuvring are available to most; physically moving at a high speed is a capability that is only available to elite athletes; and flight is available to none. As technology stands at the moment, none of these perceptual attributes translates completely to the virtual, though many of the mobility aspects are enhanced. As the resolution of images improves, and as haptic interfaces are developed, the degrees to which perceptual immersion can be achieved will increase.

Psychological and perceptual immersion in physical, virtual and augmented realities

While perceptual immersion is the normal state of affairs in the physical world, psychological immersion is not always a given. We can lose awareness of our surroundings; for example, remaining psychologically immersed during a several-hours-long meeting requires a strong act of will as the tendency is for one's mind to withdraw from the surroundings. In fact, for some activities the ability to remove our consciousness from our surroundings is a prerequisite; if we cannot ignore those around us when watching a film we are less likely to become emotionally connected to the narrative. The zero sum of attention that Sadowski and Stanney (2002) refer to when becoming psychologically immersed in digital spaces makes necessary the idea that we 'depart' from the physical, in order to 'arrive' at the virtual. However, our ability to become psychologically immersed in the virtual world always requires an engagement of belief in the authenticity of the computer-generated world – the more so, the less perceptually immersive it is; whereas for most physical world locations this is not the case. However, there are some physical spaces that do require at least some suspension of disbelief to become fully immersed in the experience. Feeling part of a performance, feeling excited by a sporting event or being moved by a spiritual location is not determined by the physical environment alone, these spaces indeed call for an engagement of belief for the participant to be truly 'part' of them.

So immersiveness is a given in the physical world, and is not (yet) complete in the virtual. Psychological immersion varies in both, but immediacy is still the domain of the physical rather than the virtual. The interfaceless technologies that are completely unobtrusive are still to arrive. Yet, in the real world, we are rarely (if ever) aware of the mediating role of the senses in conveying information to us, unless an impairment in our vision or hearing intervenes. Throughout this book, however, we have distinguished between immediacy and psychological immersion. We noted that the latter happens independently of perceptual immersion, in that some perceived mediations can detract from a feeling of psychological immersion while others can enhance it. The interface can be overwhelming (as the disaster management students found when viewing virtual notecards in Chapter 8), but it can also support the user in being immersed psychologically in the experience. For example, way-finding in virtual worlds using maps on the screen can enable users to feel more part of the environment, despite the fact that this information is a visible layer between the viewer and the space. When exploring the theatres in Theatron3,[1] the paradata available to students made sense of that space for them, and provided additional context. The ability of the user to adapt to technology, to develop an unconscious competency at sense-making, using these pop-up boxes and clickable menus, means that, once accustomed to them, the interface (although perceived) becomes non-intrusive. It simply turns into another sense, through which the virtual is experienced.

With the advent of AR, the affordances of the virtual world are being imported to the physical. Through the use of devices such as Google Glass (wearable AR spectacles), the physical world will no longer be interfaceless. Like the virtual worlds' viewers, although intrusive at first, the heads-up displays and available paradata will become second nature as we adapt to their use. This technology will enable us, for example, to see a real-time historical site placed in a cultural context with relevant information displayed instantly in front of our eyes, forming the signifying system in semiotic social spaces. Rather than then being alienating spaces, in which information is not communicated and the lack of knowledge of boundary objects precludes full understanding of them, the paradata added via AR act as boundary spanners to enable full participation in the space. Therefore, in the same way that accompanying interfaces can help in making the virtual world more psychologically immersive, AR has the potential to do the same in the physical world. With paradata being part of our perception of the surroundings, the immediacy is decreased; however, we connect to these places much more through a greater understanding of the significance of the elements of the environment, through greater abilities to way-find, and through being able to place that space in a wider historical and geographical context. Thus the degree of psychological immersion is increased.

Learning in virtual worlds

In 1964, Marshall McLuhan stated that '[U]nder electric technology the entire business of man becomes learning and knowing' (McLuhan, 1964: 69). New media technologies are indeed responsible for shifting the emphasis of the study process towards a more visual, customizable and, as a result, more enjoyable experience. Such processes as accessing resources, analysing data and storing files are increasingly technology-heavy. Hypermedia and hypertext enable interactivity of virtually any study content, promoting a more personalized approach for each learner (Kuksa, 2008a: 75). Virtual worlds provide opportunities to learn about a variety of subjects, including sensitive and practically difficult subjects, such as experiencing other cultures or environments in a safe setting (Steventon et al., 2008; King and Fouts, 2009). These spaces also welcome people with disabilities, or people who are geographically isolated, or those who due to their sexuality or ethnicity may suffer from prejudice that will prevent them from learning and interacting as equals with others. Contemporary futurists (such as, for example, William Crossman) predict that the emergence of talking computers will make the keyboard and the mouse redundant, and relatively soon non-literate learners will be able to educate themselves through much-improved speech recognition technologies, using on-screen intelligent agents.

Even with current technology, the opportunity to acquire knowledge via, for example, virtual heritage sites brings a flavour of active exploration in a hunt for information, often tailoring the experience to one's educational background and previous awareness of the subject. The addition of paradata to 3D reconstructions adds important facts and context to the builds in virtual worlds. More importantly, however, paradata underline the academic underpinnings of the creation of the site, complementing the 'wow' factor noted by Richard Beacham (2011), and making transparent the occasional conflicting views about how the original structures actually appeared, since (as noted in Chapter 3) these vary in degrees of credibility. The inherent problem from an educational perspective is that once a single version of a 3D model is chosen from the range of available interpretations, it has a sense of reality in the mind of the onlooker. No matter how the uncertainty in the model is accentuated, for example by using different colours to present different degrees of credibility (suggested by Jones, 2008), this still happens. The ability to place paradata in a specific location in virtual worlds and, through augmented reality, in the physical world, where it can make the most contextual sense, is a remarkable learning tool. Integrating the 'physical' reality of the structure with the information explaining how it was built brings space and text together, enhancing the meaning of both. Using virtual spaces for educational purposes does not only mean learning about the spaces *per se*, it can also mean learning about experiencing them. In Chapter 5 we discussed how, in order to transform a peripheral and disconnected view of on-screen events into a fully immersive 'space' voyage, the emotional connection with that space is needed. To perceive one's avatar standing on a stage in the round, or at the focus of a huge amphitheatre as an emotional experience, or to understand that a certain virtual space is an integral part of a larger culture (such as Renaissance Island, or Caledon, or the Isle of Wyrms), requires the learner to develop a sense of inhabitation. If we want our students to be able to engage at that level, and to give them the emotional domain that makes experiential learning so effective, then we must allow them to explore, to communicate and to be *moved* by their time in a virtual world.

There are design elements that can help achieve this. For example, inserting a variety of media and paying attention to such details as textures and sounds (or even collapsed buildings and dead bodies, as indicated by the disaster management students in Chapter 8) that signify an internal reality to the space could heighten the emotional content. Furthermore, designing educational scenarios is a key component of any learning activity. In virtual worlds, the two most widely accepted scenarios are an exact replication of a real-world exercise or a simulation of only the most relevant aspects. The SWIFT project[2] is a good example of the latter scenario. This study, which took place at the University of

Leicester, considers simulated rather than replicated spaces for developing immersive learning activities in Second Life for students studying genetics. The reason for this is that it is very difficult to replicate accurately the tactile and visual impression of interacting with the physical laboratory equipment, but also that the aim of the experience is to enable learners to explore, experiment and assess various situations and processes in a risk-free environment. Furthermore, the stages of genetic sampling and analysis are accompanied by animations of chemical reactions within the virtual world, prioritizing educational content over immediacy and realism. There are also activities designed specifically for virtual worlds, such as game-based learning tasks, which, as some researchers argue, help the learner to become *a creative professional*. In 2006, David Williamson Shaffer wrote that conventional education methods are 'busy preparing students for the commodity jobs of the past – jobs that will be long gone by the time they finish school' (2006: 4). He argues that learning creatively by using technology and, in particular, computer games, is crucial to survival in the new global competition for innovative work. There are supporters of Shaffer's 'epistemic' framework, but there are also critics who state that the problem with game-based learning is that the students are getting very good at playing a particular game, but not at learning in general. Indeed, the field of game-based learning is still under investigation. Most educators, however, tend to agree that current mainstream learning environments need to be changed and, in fact, are changing and becoming increasingly hybridized, extended and mixed (Savin-Baden, 2013: 72).

Underlying all of this, though, is the same number one rule as with any learning task. The design of the activity, its purpose and value to the recipient, as well as its alignment with the other learning undertaken, will all promote greater motivation on the part of the student to become involved. This, however, should be demonstrated directly to the learners, not simply assumed that this is self-evident. No matter how technically brilliant the technology is, or how much a fan of virtual worlds a student has become, a learning activity will still not be effective if the recipients cannot see the point of it.

Communicating history in virtual worlds

There is a range of challenges to presenting history to people. Artefacts need to be protected and preserved, so, more often than not, they are seen in display cases rather than *in situ* where their context and function can be more fully appreciated. The spaces and the objects associated with any artefact or cultural heritage site have a wealth of narratives, background history and influences. These paradata, however, are often unlinked (for example, by being placed on a billboard in the corner of a room) from the conventional exhibition spaces in which they have most meaning. Furthermore, such issues as mobility and access can prevent a number of people from experiencing history first hand, either because of the disabilities of the viewers or because of the remote location of the site or its fragility. Or, sometimes, the site no longer exists. The tangible, technical and material history is represented mainly through the authoritarian lens of conventional museological approaches, which privilege certain narratives and perspectives. There is a growing need, however, to move away from the vertical system of the 'Authorised Heritage Discourse' (Smith, 2006) to the horizontal, levelled, democratic system of multi-vocal, multi-viewpoint discourses and epistemologies. Such a post-structural approach to preserving history does not privilege a single authoritative discourse and is particularly valuable for providing access to and inclusion of intangible heritages, such as the often undocumented, or casually noted, social histories of families and communities, vital to the formation and understanding of identity. It seeks to dismantle unidirectional, authorial practice in display and interpretation and recognizes the value in creating stable archives of plural histories, and, furthermore, promotes genuinely interactive participation in which artefact, text and memory are authored by the content users – the participants. Rapid developments in technology create obsolescence and therefore potential loss of access. Family artefacts, such as still and moving images, sound recordings and documents may be lost forever if technology preservation issues are not addressed. The commonly practised 'biscuit tin' approach to the archiving of undated and unidentified family snapshots may make sense while there are still people present to contextualize the images, but how can they be comprehended by future generations? As discussed above, the virtual presence agenda promoted by the majority of art institutions and venues brought into question the sustainability of digitized artefacts, exhibitions and cultural sites. The term 'digital footprint' has emerged to describe the use of energy and the production of carbon dioxide for generating and delivering digital products. And this problem, though still poorly understood due to the complexity of the World Wide Web, raises concerns about the standards of digital preservation, and, furthermore, about who is responsible for this environmental impact – technology or service providers, the networks, or the users of cultural heritage sites? As we move increasingly towards using virtual spaces for preserving, studying and displaying historical artefacts and for reconstructing past events, as well as towards more physical heritage sites using AR to make their history more meaningful and accessible to contemporary audiences, will history itself become a more fluid concept?

Virtual worlds (and AR) can help in facilitating the post-structural approach to preserving histories by placing their disparate elements in the most meaningful settings, with the sum of information being greater than the whole. Besides this, they help to redefine what our notion of history actually is. Understanding what translates from the physical world to the virtual, when buildings (with which we have a historical relationship) are reproduced digitally, leads to questions about how our experiences become associated with that newly generated space. In part, these new virtual builds may recall our own personal connection with their physical versions, but our emotional link with the reconstructed space is probably not that strong if we are just observing it within the virtual world. It is possible, however, to imbue virtual spaces with their own history. It could be done, for example, through the design of activities, such as in Ian Upton's *Ritual Circles*, to foster these experiences, or/and through the actions of people exploring, using and attributing meaning to those spaces under their own auspices. The different nature of the various Globe theatres within Second Life is testament to that. We discovered that some of them, though less historically accurate, are located within spaces that serve a role-play community and thus have a historical significance to that community in which they are embedded. Others, which are historically accurate, survive as showcases of the building skills and interests of their creators, and some of them are no longer in Second Life and exist only as 3D models and photographs.

In addition to exploring existing histories, residents of virtual worlds are constantly creating new communities and cultural identities, often finding more kinship inworld with others from other countries than with the offline people from their own geographical location. So does this mean that virtual worlds are also redefining our interpretation of what constitutes community and collective identity? As people modify the augmented aspect of buildings through their own adding of geotagged paradata, will this action be considered part of the intrinsic historical meaning of a site (in the same way that Banksy's street art pieces are preserved and lauded), or will it be merely ephemeral or a nuisance? Does this mean that communities will be able to create their own historical records within systems that will ensure accessibility for current and future generations? There are certainly research projects that investigate this possibility. Finally, as different applications layer different paradata onto sites, will the history of spaces diverge, depending on whether you follow an Apple or an Android historical perspective? Time will tell.

Communicating performance in virtual worlds

Theatre in virtual worlds is a developing art form. It extends the notion and experience of performance spaces by offering not only new ways of interaction, but also a place in which people can explore identity, or create new societies, new communities and even new bodies. Theatre provides a medium for exploring these new changes and challenges in the virtual world as it has always done in the physical (Kuksa and Childs, 2010). For example, the provision of opportunities to explore self-expression and creativity can be limited for some sections of our society, either because the spaces in which they can reach a desired audience are not appropriate, or because the physical world itself presents barriers to such interactions. Through exploring the potential of virtual worlds as platforms for creating social theatre and reaching out to a wider community, it is possible to overcome at least some of these obstacles. In Chapter 9 we gave centre stage to creative practitioners who belong to a growing movement of virtual theatre-makers voicing their experiences of role-playing, identity, place and character creation in virtual spaces. Second Life has become a popular environment for presenting theatre that is accessible to a broad variety of people. It enables unique theatrical performances, which take advantage of the virtual world affordances to conquer realism and real-life barriers such as gravity. The wider community working in theatre, however, is not fully aware of such work and innovation. There are also conventions around what constitutes 'real' or authentic experience of a space, interaction or, in fact, communication. Often mainstream theatre and performance academics (and also practitioners) do not include virtual world theatre in their views of what creates the legitimate domain of the field. In this book, we have attempted to counteract such preconceptions. The thesis here is that not only are virtual spaces real to those practitioners who choose them as creative platforms, they also reinvent social conventions and audience–performer relationships. On a more pragmatic level, although there are costs involved in creating spaces within virtual worlds, compared to the expenses of doing the same in the real world, they are considerably lower. The Theatrebase project discussed in Chapter 1 is a good example of how greatly the time and labour spent on rebuilding the sets on-site could be reduced through the use of virtual spaces to test different set-ups before the production is actually on tour.

It was argued in Chapter 9 that the experience of virtual worlds is akin to those of physical worlds, with the difference between the way they are performed being no greater than when a production is taken (and adopted) from one physical space to another. Performance, at its heart, is about the relationship between the actors and the spectators, and within the physical world this is made more complex through the existence of different types of performance space. The traditional theatre venue is familiar to visitors and has a set of social conventions of which the audience is aware. Even the actual act of going to the theatre has a performance element to it. Within site-specific and found spaces, however, these conventions are less familiar and need to be structured and explained to the spectators before the actual performance takes place. These spaces, in themselves, may attract some theatregoers and repel others. Within the virtual world these distinctions carry over, with 'traditionally built' theatre spaces requiring quite similar ways of behaviour and etiquette from their audiences as their physical world equivalents, whereas more non-traditional theatre venues need careful tutoring on the role of a spectator within them. The technological aspects also add an additional burden to the audiences' appreciation of the experience and the subtle training to which they need to be exposed. Despite this, however, virtual theatregoers (as noted by Gameela Wright in Chapter 9) are quite unbiased in their expectations, flexible and open to change. In some cases, they are responsible for binding the narrative of a virtual performance together or even for building a set for it. These interventions create a challenge for digital scenery designers, who more than ever need to focus on generating time-based flexible spaces, driven by a storyline. Liquid sets, and such available interaction options in Second Life as text chat and animation, produce a new non-verbal layer to communication (as noted by Ze Moo, an 'information artist' and live media consultant). Acting in the virtual world is not as straightforward as in the physical. The fact that neither actor nor spectator avatars have facial expressions could be quite disconcerting at the beginning, but the very fact that live stand-up comedy is quite popular in Second Life indicates that the users (both artists and viewers) developed a new performative language specific to this environment.

The truth is that we cannot experience theatre in the same way in the virtual world as we do in the physical, but we can abstract the key elements that make performance meaningful for us, and use those in taking something from the source reality and translating it to the target reality. Through this process, some elements may be lost, but it is also possible that we learn something new about the essential nature of theatre; aiming to understand what is it that remains when bodies, touch and other sensations are stripped away. We may choose to go for direct or indirect translation, depending on what our goals are. For example, the scale of the Theatron^3 Project's theatres in Second Life caused some discussion among the creators. Most theatres in Second Life are built to a larger scale, since avatars are often oversized and the camera position (via which the user views the virtual world) is above and slightly behind each of them. This means that viewpoints are often blocked if the ceiling is in an accurate (same as in the real world) position. The Theatron^3 models are used for teaching and research, thus the decision was to go for accuracy. So that avatars were still able to fit inside the buildings, the project offered smaller-scale forms (with a different camera position) to users. However, the performers and others who used the theatres for their creative practice tended to keep their original avatars, choosing instead to shrink them to fit within the settings against a height measure provided. This requirement to modify the avatars to some extent acted against the sense of inhabiting the space, since the users had a form that was unfamiliar to them, reducing their feeling of embodiment.

Both direct and indirect translations are equally valid, but recodification from one reality to another forces that choice upon the translator. Making explicit the problems with translation is possible within a virtual world by highlighting these with paradata in the same way that a language translator may augment the translation of a text with annotations. Though this adds to understanding and engagement, this process reduces immersion.

As could be seen from our discussion, virtual performance is a mix of disciplines, including drama, visual arts, film, architecture and public intervention. However, the question of whether this *is* performance or not can (we would assert) be dismissed. That an audience feels co-present with the actors, that they can be entertained or moved, is beyond question. The absence of a physical body sharing a physical space with other physical bodies is not crucial when avatars can be felt as adequate stand-ins. What survives is the spontaneity and the potential for variation which come with a live event. An audience member who has that sense of inhabiting the space is caught up with the performance. That aspect continues with the transition from one reality to the other.

It feels appropriate to end this section with the quote by Andrew Eglinton, who runs London Theatre Blog:

> [T]he 'real-time' web is prime territory for artistic exploration. Its structure is defined, in part, by the applications/platforms that facilitate seamless, live communication using all digital media. Its constitution is forged by the individual and the personal narratives that s/he creates as the sum of activities across these platforms. Each 'activity' is recordable, reproducible and forms a digital 'artefact'. Combined, these artefacts constitute the basis of an emerging culture – borderless, transient and democratised.
>
> (Eglinton, 2009)

Is the future 'phyrtual'?

Some users of virtual worlds, who are also keen theatregoers, reveal that moving from a non-theatrical space to a theatrical space is a greater experience of transition than that between the physical and the virtual worlds. The moment we enter the fourth place of theatre, we know that we will be called on to engage our belief in the narrative, the performance and the setting. We reduce our presence in the 'here and now' and adopt the role of a pure observer (unless we are expected to be a spectagonist). We acquire the boundary objects that require our participation, a ticket and a programme. We feel the heightened sense of import of the events, because of the shared feeling of communitas with the other audience members. We do all this not necessarily to achieve an end, but intrinsically for the act of transformation in itself. Entering the space signifies that the change is about to commence, but this is only the first step in the process, as it is demarcated temporally by the orchestra playing and the curtain rising. By contrast, the sense that we are arriving at a different space when we go online is not, perhaps, so discontinuous, as Ian Upton describes in this supplement to his contribution to Chapter 9: 'the boundaries of where you are, your presence, expand out. I have got my mobile telephone. I have got my web presence. I have got Second Life.' We are used to not simply existing as physical beings; our bodies are constantly extended throughout the virtual. We do not live physically *or* virtually, but both at the same time. We are creatures of meat, metal and code, as Stelarc articulates. We are 'phyrtual'.

Our life as phyrtual beings will become more evident as the two worlds come to be more enmeshed. With the help of AR, the mingling of avatars and physical bodies (as pioneered in the *Extract/Insert* installation) will become more commonplace. The worlds through which we move will become tagged with paradata, and the wider psychological immersion that comes with understanding a space will become greater. Such development will have a bigger impact, potentially, in those fourth places within the physical world. Places of ritual significance, performance and game spaces are all those that possess greater semiotic prominence and benefit from having that wealth of meaning made manifest. As paradata are tagged to the artefacts and people around us, the boundary objects become more accessible and the other members in our communities come to be more known to us. If we can manipulate the paradata through which we describe ourselves to others, identity becomes more malleable and role-play more attainable. As the affordances of both worlds collide and create a new synthesis, potentially new types of spaces will arise, with new conventions and new ways to communicate. Those of us who are capable will live constantly in a state of metaxis. Those who cannot adapt to the phyrtual will become increasingly alienated and isolated.

Even today, the phyrtuality of our existence triggers certain codes of behaviour which have become firmly integrated in our daily routines. Massively multi-player online role-playing games (or MMORPGs), for example, are increasingly popular and attract millions of subscribers. Despite this, however, digital exclusion is still very much of an issue in both developed and developing countries. Elderly people, people with a disability or those who due to their geographical location or political and economic circumstances are not able to connect to the Internet, are all missing out on accessing better (and cheaper) services, advanced information and knowledge. According to the Carnegie UK Trust report 'Across the divide', 'a lack of Internet access will increasingly come to represent both a symptom and a cause of poverty' (White, 2013: 4), which runs alongside a lack of confidence and skill in using digital technology. For the moment, making that step into the virtual is, at least for most of us, a step into a different space. The rules are different, our bodies are different; our identities, relationships and communities are often unlike those in real life. Besides, virtual spaces must not only be navigated but also experienced and inhabited if we are to make the most of them in our search for knowledge, in our ambition to perform, and in our online and inworld lives. Learning how to decipher these spaces, and how to communicate meaning within and through them, is not only essential for our effective use of virtual worlds, it will also prepare us for new ways of making sense of the physical reality, and of the new types of spaces that will arise. We are living in the era of digital Darwinism, when technology and society are evolving faster than the ability of many institutions, organizations and also individuals to adapt. But, ultimately, as Charles Darwin wrote in *On the Origin of Species*: '[I]n the struggle for survival, the fittest win out at the expense of their rivals because they succeed in adapting themselves best to their environment.' In order to survive to be phyrtual, we must adapt. Those who do not will be left outside the new spaces. The rest of us will inhabit them.

Notes

1. *http://cms.cch.kcl.ac.uk/theatron/.*
2. *http://www2.le.ac.uk/projects/swift.*

Glossary

Activity Theory is a framework, in the essence of which lies the notion that an activity can be represented as the action of a subject on an object, but this will always be mediated through the employment of an external artefact. It was originally formulated in Russia in the 1920s by Lev Vygotsky and further developed in the 1990s by Yrjö Engeström. This book presents a further extension of Activity Theory by incorporating the identity of the subject and the situated experience of the setting of the activity within its framework.

Affinity space is a particular type of a semiotic social space, which hosts individuals engaged in a common activity.

Agents are graphical personifications of computer software processes, able to learn the users' preferences and interests, make suggestions, function with minimal supervision and customize their assistance.

Augmented reality (AR) is a way of viewing digital information by superimposing it onto a real-life physical environment in front of the participants. The AR users can see the real and virtual world simultaneously, meaning that instead of blocking the real environment the computer 'overwrites' and comments on what a spectator sees. AR offers a *hypermediated* experience, where its users are very much aware of computer graphics as a medium.

Avatars are graphical representations of a user, under their direct control within a virtual environment. Avatars can either be 2D (an icon in online forums) or 3D (an animated character in computer games and virtual world communities). 3D avatars enable the projection of identity within the virtual environment and provide a locus for position-sensitive interactions.

Buff is a verb (in gaming) which means to add additional health or strength or mana (a sort of magical energy) to team-mates.

Communitas is a Latin noun which refers to a mental state in which one is able to free him-/herself of the constraints of normal life and set aside social and personal differences, resulting in a greater feeling of unity, which can occur in secular and sacred spaces. Victor Turner defined this term as the heightened sense of belonging that occurs within a group when sharing a common purpose and activity.

Communities of Practice is a framework, developed by cognitive anthropologists Etienne Wenger and Jean Lave in 1991, for describing the process by which an individual's participation (personal and professional) in a community can develop, and the ways in which the community itself can evolve.

Cultural presence is the concept introduced by Erik Champion in 2005 which links together virtual reality and cultural heritage. It combines the notion of 'being there' with the communicational, social and contextual goals of heritage through the addition of symbolism, the explicit expression of self-identity and learning.

Cyberspace is the global information and communication infrastructure which is generally considered to have two branches: computer networks and electronic storage technologies, and 3D virtual worlds.

Dasein is the term used by Martin Heidegger to describe the experience of 'being', and translates as literally 'being there'. It could be described as a foreshadowing of the current definition of psychological immersion. It has defied specific interpretation by philosophers, but is generally thought to be an attempt to distinguish between simply being situated in a space and being located in a place; with our sense of being influenced by our relationship to our surroundings.

Digitality is the instantaneous communication, global connectivity and ubiquitous media that are in charge of almost every aspect of our everyday lives. It refers to the capabilities of a particular technology and the way we think about it, combining both technical and creative components and stimulating continuous technological evolution.

Disclosurists are people who feel the need to get to know the 'real' offline identity of the person with whom they are interacting online. For disclosurists, interacting with only the pseudonymous online identities feels inauthentic. The significance in Case 8.1 of disclosurists not feeling psychological immersion is that this indicates that they are not experiencing embodiment in online interactions, resulting in a sense of unreality when conducting them.

Engagement (within the specific terminology used in this book) is the critical reflection possible when standing apart from a text, or a game, and is taken from the usage employed by Diane Carr.

Flow is a concept originated by Mihaly Csíkszentmihályi, which describes a state in which attention is heightened, and goals, action and the environment are all aligned.

Fourth place is a term coined in this book by Mark Childs and is an extension of Oldenburg's first, second and third places typology. It is an attempt to blend the work of Gee, Turner, Huizinga and others to identify the specific qualities of places (both physical and virtual) which require the willing suspension of disbelief to be fully engaged with.

Fourth wall in theatre terminology is the invisible frontier that divides the stage and the audience into two clearly perceptible parts.

Gesamtkunstwerk is a concept associated with Richard Wagner's aesthetic ideals for defining drama as the ideal medium, which unites all separate branches of art including music, architecture, painting, poetry and dance and embraces them in the 'collective artwork' and the 'synthesis of the arts'.

Hypermediacy refers to the perception of the technology that is mediating our experience. This is not necessarily an impediment to the experience; however, the awareness of the tools that act as mediators can sometimes be deliberate and instructive.

Immediacy is a style of visual representation the goal of which is to make the viewer disregard the presence of the medium. For the purposes of this book, it is defined as 'the perception of non-mediation' when a technology mediates an experience. All technologies intrude into the experience to some extent, so immediacy is never total. Interfaceless technologies have greater immediacy, as do those that are immersive.

Immersiveness is the objective measure of the vividness (or realism) of the technology, and the degree of interactivity that contributes to perceptual immersion. The distinction is made here, though, that immersiveness does not *cause* perceptual immersion since this is a product of the individual's perception; immersive technologies merely provide the opportunity (to varying degrees) of enabling this perception to take place.

Interactivity is an attribute of any representational media that enables a two-way communication between a source of information and a user who can initiate or respond to queries. It is comprised of manipulability, responsiveness and reciprocation. *Manipulability* is the extent to which a participant can change the environment, both in terms of the fineness of the changes and the range of elements that can be changed. *Reciprocation* is the degree of feedback from the environment about the changes made, whether from objects or other users within the environment. *Responsiveness* refers to the speed of the feedback, rather than the degree to which it takes place. An environment which is more manipulable and with a range of immediate sensory feedback will be more immersive.

Limen is the threshold of a physiological or psychological response. *Liminality* can be spatial (when, for example, the edge of a stage separates the imaginary world of the actors from the audience) and temporal (when, for example, a regular space is transformed into ritual).

Liminal is a term used by Victor Turner to describe the threshold between the space of normal experience and the space in which rituals occur; this can also apply to any structured formal space with a heightened semiotic system, such as theatres or games, but since these are usually less formal and structured Turner describes these as *liminoid.*

Machinima is the process of making real-time animated films by utilizing the 3D graphics technology of immersive virtual worlds such as computer games.

Metadata is a term meaning data about data. For example, if data exists in the form of an image, or text, then the metadata will describe the author, the date the image or text was created, and who uploaded the metadata. British Library cataloguing information in the front part of a book is a familiar form of metadata.

Metaxis is the word used by Plato to describe the condition of 'in-betweenness' applied to spirituality as a location between the human and the divine. It is a state of belonging to two autonomous worlds at the same time, which is applicable to performance studies when the actors go in and out of character. In this book it refers to the switching between the states of critical engagement and immersion and describes the sense of being both in the physical world and the virtual world simultaneously, or switching back and forth between the two.

Mixed reality (**MR**) refers to the display technology which combines real and virtual environments.

Newb (or newbie) is the term used to describe someone who is new to an experience or an environment, often a technologically-based one. It differs from the term *noob*, or *n00b*, in that, whereas a newb is understandably and acceptably unfamiliar with the codes and mores of their new situation, they accept their new status and attempt to learn. A noob, on the other hand, is oblivious to social conventions and makes little attempt to mitigate the effect that their presence as a new person may have on others.

New Institutionalism is a term borrowed from economics and sociology to describe the process of art curators taking charge of a significant number of venues to concentrate on a social democratic axis and establishing dialogical engagement with a community in north-central Europe.

OpenSim (or OpenSimulator) is an open source multi-platform, multi-user 3D application server. It can be used to create a virtual environment (or world) which can be accessed through a variety of clients, on multiple protocols (*http://opensimulator.org/wiki/Main_Page*).

Paradata are additional data that accompany data that provide context, explanatory information, supplementary resources and even (in an educational context) materials to assess learning. In a virtual building paradata could be photographs of the physical build, the history of the site, or alternative theories of how the building may have existed.

Perceptual immersion is an aspect of immersion – the degree to which 'what you see' submerges the perceptual system of the user, enabling the user to disregard the medium. The greater the immersiveness of the technology is, the greater the chances for perceptual immersion to be experienced. However, this also depends to some extent on the ability and experience of the viewer to perceive and make sense of the technologies they see, hear or touch.

Presence is the natural perception of an environment. It is variously (and inconsistently) defined by the literature, sometimes being used as simply a shortened form of telepresence, and on other occasions being equated to the experience of 'being there' at a remote or virtual location. Within the extended Activity Theory model presented in this book, and the writings of the authors, presence is divided into four aspects: 1) 'mediated presence', equivalent to the experience of 'being there' or psychological immersion; 2) social presence, the ability to project and perceive others within the environment; 3) co-presence, the sense that one is sharing the environment with another person; and 4) self-presence or embodiment, the sense that one's self has a reality within that environment.

Psychological immersion is an aspect of immersion – the sense of submergence in a space that is not one's immediate physical environment. It is also the sense of being subsumed within a technology, or medium, due to a high level of perceptual immersion, which is (in its turn) caused by a range of other factors (e.g., a narrative). The motivation of the participant also has a contributory effect.

Remediation is the formal logic by which new media refashion prior media forms, and along with immediacy and hypermediacy it is one of the three traits of the genealogy of new media proposed in 1999 by Jay David Bolter and Richard Grusin.

Rezzing is the term used in Second Life to describe the process of creating a new object via the edit window or by dragging an existing object from a resident's inventory. It was adopted from the film, *Tron* (1982, Walt Disney Productions), in which the verb 'de-rezz' means to dissolve in a certain way.

Second Life is a trademark of Linden Lab. It is a virtual land space, consisting of a few continents and many small islands, which dominates much of the social activity and educational practices 'behind the computer screen'. It was launched publicly in 2005 by Linden Lab and is hosted on their servers. The users of Second Life interact with each other through avatars. To date, it has approximately 1 million regular accounts (the precise number of users is not known since people may have more than one account). At its peak, Second Life had around 1.4 million users.

Semiotic social spaces (SSSes) is a concept developed by James Paul Gee. An SSS is a space which has a specific signifying system associated with it, and which can be physical (a classroom or an art gallery) or online (a chatroom or a game).

Steampunk is a subgenre of science fiction set in a parallel world which represents a high-tech Victorian British Empire.

Tank is a type of character played in gaming that absorbs a lot of damage, either because of strength or armour, and therefore will act to protect the other players by attracting and absorbing attacks. To **buff** a tank, therefore, means to add additional strength or vitality to a player who has borne the brunt of an attack and is therefore ailing.

Telepresence is inconsistently defined in the literature. This book returns to its original formulation by Marvin Minsky, in that it not only refers to the idea of experiencing a remote location as if 'being there', by viewing it remotely, but also by being able to interact and operate at distance.

Translation is the taking of ideas from one language and converting them to another through a process of abstraction (from the original language) and recodification (into the target language). However, most ideas are not precisely translatable since they make complete sense only within the context of the original. The choices for a translator are: 1) to limit translations to those that are directly possible; 2) to choose an indirect translation as an incomplete translation; or 3) to indirectly translate and accompany that translation with paradata. This last choice increases understanding and engagement but reduces psychological immersion. In Part 3 of this book, the transfer of spaces from the physical world to the virtual world is equated with this process.

Virtual environment is defined in this book as any online networked platform, including simple web pages.

Virtual reality (VR) is a computer simulation of a real or imaginary system that enables users to perform operations in virtual spaces, and shows effects in real time. It is part of **cyberspace**.

Virtual reality monitoring is the decision process in which participants distinguish between real, virtual and imagined events.

Virtual space is defined in this book as a part of any online networked environment in which a metaphorical space can be used for interaction, including chatrooms, discussion boards or social networking sites.

Virtual worlds are defined in this book as online networked environments which are a navigable 2D or 3D space, which are persistent, and in which users take on digital representations in order to interact. Second Life and *World of Warcraft* are examples of virtual worlds.

Vividness (or realness) is the degree of realism of the technology. In this book it is defined as the function of both: 1) the range of senses across which the environment carries information (the breadth); and 2) the degree of definition of any of those channels (the depth). Thus, a technology that has a higher dpi, or that offers haptic feedback, or more frames per second, is considered more 'real' than one which does not. Realness and interactivity, in combination, contribute to **immersiveness.**

Web 1.0/2.0/3.0 are all different iterations (generations) of the World Wide Web. Web 1.0 is a structure of hyperlinked text and images stored on different computers to create a single seamless system of information. This was developed by Tim Berners-Lee while at CERN from 1989 to 1991. Web 2.0 is a term invented by Tim O'Reilly in 1999 to describe the more participative form into which the WWW had evolved. Web 3.0 refers to the further development of the web to have a semantic organizing structure. To use the example of planning an evening out: a Web 1.0 interaction would present information about local cinemas and restaurants, on websites created by those companies; a Web 2.0 interaction would include reviews and ratings by previous customers and audiences; a Web 3.0 interaction would store information about your preferences and pre-select a potential set of activities based on those previous interactions.

Web 4.0 (the 'Symbiotic Web') is the predicted fourth generation of the WWW, which will be able to communicate with us like we communicate with each other.

Willing suspension of disbelief refers to the willingness of the viewer to disregard the limitations of a medium. It is the intent on the part of the viewer, reader or participant in a fourth place to take on the mores, social conventions, belief structures and goals of that environment, and momentarily depart from those of the outside world. This is a process that Carrie Heeter more accurately describes as an 'engagement of belief'. The motivation for this may be the experience of **communitas** that occurs when sharing the space with others also engaging their belief, or the sense of **flow** and psychological moratorium that can occur within these environments, or because it is fun.

References

http://www.londoncharter.org/.
http://www.michael-culture.eu/.
http://www.minervaeurope.org/.
http://museumscomputergroup.org.uk/about/.
http://opera.media.mit.edu/projects/deathandthepowers/index.php.

Allbeck, J.M. and Badler, N.I. (2002) Embodied autonomous agents. In K.M. Stanney (ed.) *Handbook of Virtual Environments: Design, Implementation and Applications* (pp. 313–2). Mahwah, NJ: Lawrence Erlbaum Associates.

Andres, A.N., Pozuelo, F.B., Marimon, J.R. and de Mesa Gisbert, A. (2012) Generation of virtual models of cultural heritage, *Journal of Cultural Heritage* 13: 103–6.

Arbaugh, J.B. and Hwang, A. (2006) Does 'teaching presence' exist in online MBA courses? *The Internet and Higher Education* 9(1): 9–21.

Aronowsky, A., Sanzenbacher, B., Childs, M., Peachey, A., Villanosa, K. et al. (2013) Promoting embodied learning through virtual and real world gaming experiences. Games+Learning+Society Conference 9.0, Madison, Wisconsin, 12–14 June.

Aronson, A. (2005) *Looking into the Abyss: Essays on Scenography*. Ann Arbor, MI: The University of Michigan Press.

Barnes, P. (1986) *A Companion to Post-War British Theatre*. Beckenham, UK: Croom Helm.

Baugh, C. (2005) *Theatre, Performance and Technology: The Development of Scenography in the Twentieth Century*. London: Palgrave Macmillan.

Beacham, R. (2011) Concerning the paradox of paradata. Or, 'I don't want *realism*; I want magic!', *Virtual Archeology Review* 2(4): 49–52.

Becker, B. and Mark, G. (2002) Social conventions in computer-mediated communication: a comparison of three online shared virtual environments. In R. Schroeder (ed.) *The Social Life of Avatars* (pp. 19–39). London: Springer-Verlag.

Begg, M., Ellaway, R., Dewhurst, D. and Macleod, H. (2007) Transforming professional healthcare narratives into structured game-informed learning activities, *Innovate* 3(6). Available from: *http://citeseerx.ist.psu.edu/viewdoc/download?doi=10.1.1.186.5122&rep=rep1&type=pdf.*

Bell, M. (2008) Toward a definition of 'virtual worlds', *Journal of Virtual Worlds Research* 1(1): 1–5.

Bennett, S. (1997) *Theatre Audiences: A Theory of Production and Reception*. London: Routledge.

Billinghurst, M. and Kato, H. (1999) Collaborative mixed reality in mixed reality merging physical world and virtual world. In *Proceedings of the International Symposium on Mixed Reality* (pp. 261–84), Yokohama, Japan, 19–21 March.

Biocca, F. (1997) The cyborg's dilemma: progressive embodiment in virtual environments, *Journal of Computer-Mediated Communication* 3(2). Available from: *http://onlinelibrary.wiley.com/doi/10.1111/j.1083-6101.1997.tb00070.x/full.*

Blake, E., Nunez, D. and Labuschagne, B. (2007) Longitudinal effects on presence: suspension of disbelief or distrust of naive belief? In *Proceedings of the 10th Annual International Workshop on Presence* (pp. 291–5), Barcelona, Spain.

Bowman, D.A. (2002) Principles for the design of performance-oriented interaction techniques. In K.M. Stanney (ed.) *Handbook of Virtual Environments: Design, Implementation and Applications* (pp. 277–300). Mahwah, NJ: Lawrence Erlbaum Associates.

Britt, A. (2008) On language: avatar, *New York Times Magazine*, 8 August.

Bogdanovych, A., Rodriguez-Aguilar, J.A., Simoff, S. and Cohen, A. (2010) Authentic interactive reenactment of cultural heritage with 3D worlds and artificial intelligence, *Applied Artificial Intelligence* 24: 617–47.

Bolter, J.D. and Grusin, R. (1999) *Remediation: Understanding New Media*. London: MIT Press.

Brook, P. (1968) *The Empty Space*. London: Penguin Group.

Bryant, R. (2001) What kind of space is cyberspace? *An Internet Journal of Philosophy* 5. Available from: *http://www.minerva.mic.ul.ie//vol5/cyberspace.html#note%201.*

Caillois, R. (1961) *Man, Play and Games*. New York: The Free Press of Glencoe.

Cameron, F. and Kenderdine, S. (eds) (2007) *Theorizing Digital Cultural Heritage: A Critical Discourse*. Cambridge, MA: MIT Press.

Carr, D. (2006) Play and pleasure. In D. Carr, D. Buckingham, A. Burn and G. Schott (eds) *Computer Games: Text Narrative and Play* (pp. 45–58). Cambridge: Polity Press.

Caspi, A. and Blau, I. (2008) Social presence in online discussion groups: testing three conceptions and their relations to perceived learning, *Social Psychology of Education* 11: 323–46.

Castronova, C. (2005) *Synthetic Worlds: The Business and Culture of Online Games*. Chicago, IL: The University of Chicago Press.

Causey, M. (1999) The screen test of the double: the uncanny performer in the space of technology, *Theatre Journal* 51(4): 383–94.

Center for Research on Activity, Development and Learning (2004) Cultural-historical activity theory (CHAT) and developmental work research (DWR). Available from: *http://www.edu.helsinki.fi/activity/pages/chatanddwr/activitysystem/*.

Champion, E. (2005) Cultural presence. In S. Dasgupta (ed.) *Encyclopaedia of Virtual Communities and Technologies* (pp. 95 101). Hershey, PA: Idea Group Reference.

Champion, E.M. (2008) Otherness of place: game-based interaction and learning in virtual heritage projects, *International Journal of Heritage Studies* 14(3): 210–28.

Cheok, A., Weihua, W., Yang, X., Prince, S., Wan, F. et al. (2002) Interactive theatre experience in embodied and wearable mixed reality space. In *Proceedings of ISMAR* (pp. 59–68).

Childs, M. (2010) A conceptual framework for mediated environments, *Educational Research* 52(2): 197–213.

Childs, M. (2011) Identity: a primer. In A. Peachey and M. Childs (eds) *Reinventing Ourselves: Exploring Identity in Virtual Worlds* (pp. 13–32). London: Springer.

Childs, M. (2012) Design for *Dasein*: personalising avatars for more effective learning. Paper presented at the Second Global Conference on Experiential Learning in Virtual Worlds, Interdisciplinary.Net, Prague, Czech Republic, 12–14 March.

Childs. M. (2013) Keeping it real? An introduction to experiential learning in virtual worlds. In M. Childs and G. Withnail (eds) *Experiential Learning in Virtual Worlds* (pp. vii–xx). Oxford: Interdisciplinary Press.

Childs, M. and Kuksa, I. (2009) 'Why are we in the floor?' Learning about theatre design in Second LifeTM. In *Proceedings of the EDULEARN09 International Conference on Education and New Learning Technologies* (pp. 1134–45), Barcelona, Spain, 6–8 July.

Childs, M. and Peachey, A. (2013) Love it or hate it: students' responses to the experience of virtual worlds. In M. Childs and G. Withnail (eds) *Experiential Learning in Virtual Worlds*. Oxford: Interdisplinary.Net.

Childs, M. and Pierpoint, S. (2010) Virtual bodies on a virtual stage: findings ways to communicate concepts of virtual performance. Paper presented at the 10th DIVERSE Conference, 6–8 July, University of Southern Maine, Portland.

Childs, M. and Rowe, K. (2009) Virtual theater history: teaching with Theatron. Paper presented at the 125th Modern Languages Association Convention, Philadelphia, 28 December 2009.

Conole, G. (2013) *Designing for Learning in an Open World*. London: Springer.

Cormier, D. (2008) Rhizomatic education: community as curriculum, *Innovate* 4(5). Available from: *http://www.innovateonline.info/index.php?view=article&id=550*.

Darken, R.P. and Peterson, B. (2002) Spatial orientation, wayfinding and representation. In K.M. Stanney (ed) *Handbook of Virtual Environments: Design, Implementation and Applications* (pp. 379–402). Mahwah, NJ: Lawrence Erlbaum Associates.

Darken, R.P. and Sibert, J.L. (1993) A toolset for navigation in virtual environments. In *Proceedings of UIST '93 (Atlanta, GA, USA)* (pp. 157–65). New York: ACM Press.

de Freitas, S. and Oliver, M. (2006) How can exploratory learning with games and simulations within the curriculum be most effectively evaluated? *Computers & Education* 46: 249–64.

Dobson, S. (2009) Remediation. Understanding new media – revisiting a classic, *Seminar.net – International Journal of Media, Technology and Lifelong Learning* 5(2). Available from: *http://www.seminar.net/index.php/reviews-hovedmeny-110/68-remediation-understanding-new-media-revisiting-a-classic*.

Dreyfus, H. (1991) *Being-in-the-World: A Commentary on Heidegger's Being and Time Division I*. Cambridge, MA: MIT Press.

Eco, U. (1962) *The Open Work*, translated by A. Cancogni. Cambridge, MA: Harvard University Press.

Edwards, A. (2004) Understanding context, understanding practice in early education, *European Early Childhood Education Research Journal* 12(1): 85–101.

Eglinton, A. (2009) Theatre in Second Life. *London Theatre Blog* (weblog), 7 February. Available from: *http://www.londontheatreblog.co.uk/theatre-in-second-life/*.

Ellison, K. and Matthes, C. (2010) Virtual history: a socially networked pedagogy of enlightenment, *Educational Research* 52(3): 297–307.

Engeström, Y. (1987) *Learning By Expanding: An Activity-Theoretical Approach To Developmental Research*. Helsinki, Finland: Orienta-Konsultit.

Ernst & Young (2010) Monetizing digital media: creating value consumers will buy. Media & Entertainment Report by EYGM Limited. Available from: *http://www.ey.com/Publication/vwLUAssets/Mon%C3%A9tiser_les_m%C3%A9dias_num%C3%A9riques/$FILE/Monetizing_digital_media.pdf*.

Ettlinger, N. (2009) Whose capitalism? Mean discourse and/or actions of the heart, *Emotion, Space and Society* 2(2): 92–7.

Fernandes, K.J., Raja, V. and Eyre, J. (2003) Cybersphere: the fully immersive spherical projection system, *Communications of the ACM* 46(9): 141–6.

Field, A. (2009) Experimental theatre is a question of space. Available from: *http://www.guardian.co.uk/stage/theatreblog/2009/sep/29/experimental-theatre-space*.

Floridi, L. (2005) The philosophy of presence: from epistemic failure to successful observation, *Presence* 14(6): 656–67.

Frawley, W. (2000) Prolegomenon to a theory of translation. In L. Venuti (ed.) *The Translation Studies Reader*. London: Routledge.

Ganesh, S., van Schie, H., de Lange, F., Thompson, E. and Wigboldus, D. (2011) How the human brain goes virtual: distinct cortical regions of the person-processing network are involved in self-identification with virtual agents, *Cerebral Cortex* 22(7): 1577–85.

Gee, J.P. (2005) Semiotic social spaces and affinity spaces: from the age of mythology to today's schools. In D. Barton and K. Tusting (eds) *Beyond Communities of Practice: Language Power and Social Context* (pp. 214–32). New York: Cambridge University Press.

Gere, C. (2002) *Digital Culture*. London: Reaktion Books.

Gibson, W. (1984) *Neuromancer*. New York: The Berkley Publishing Group.

Gillen, J., Ferguson, R., Peachey, A. and Twining, P. (2013) Seeking planning permission to build a gothic cathedral on a virtual island. In G. Merchant, J. Gillen, J. Marsh and J. Davies (eds) *Virtual Literacies: Interactive Spaces for Children and Young People* (pp. 190–207). New York: Routledge.

Goel, A.K., Vattam, S., Wiltgen, B. and Helms, M. (2012) Cognitive, collaborative, conceptual and creative – four characteristics of the next generation of knowledge-based CAD systems: a study in biologically inspired design, *Computer-Aided Design* 44: 879–900.

Goldberg, K. (2000) The unique phenomenon of a distance. In K. Goldberg (ed.) *The Robot in the Garden: Telerobotics and Telepistemology in the Age of the Internet* (pp. 2–20). Cambridge, MA: MIT Press.

Grau, O. (2003) *Virtual Art: From Illusion to Immersion*. London: The MIT Press.

Hall, S. (1980) Cultural studies: two paradigms, *Media, Culture and Society* (2): 57–72.

Heeter, C. (1995) Communication research on consumer VR. In F. Biocca and M.R. Levy (eds) *Communication in the Age of Virtual Reality* (pp. 191–218). Hillsdale, NJ: Lawrence Erlbaum Associates.

Hermon, S. (2008) Reasoning in 3D: a critical appraisal of the role of 3D modelling and virtual reconstructions in archaeology. In B. Frischer and A. Dakouri-Hild (eds) *Beyond Illustration: 2D and 3D Digital Technologies as Tools for Discovery in Archaeology* (pp. 36–45). Oxford: Archaeopress.

Hermon, S. and Kalisperis, L. (2011) Between the real and the virtual: 3D visualization in the cultural heritage domain – expectations and prospects, *Virtual Archeology Review* 2(4): 59–63.

Herold, D.K. (2010) Mediating media studies – simulating critical awareness in a virtual environment, *Computers & Education* 54: 791–8.

Hodder, I. and Cessford, C. (2004) Daily practice and social memory at Çatalhöyük, *American Antiquity* 69(1): 17–40.

Hoffman, H.G., Garcia-Palacios, A., Ayanna, K., Thomas, A.K. and Schmidt, A. (2001) Virtual reality monitoring: phenomenal characteristics of real, virtual, and false memories, *CyberPsychology and Behaviour* 4(5): 565–72.

Huizinga, J. (1970) *Homo Ludens*. London: Routledge and Kegan Paul. (Originally published in 1938.)

Ibanez, J. and Delgado-Mata, C. (2011) Lessons from research on interaction with virtual environments, *Journal of Network and Computer Applications* 34: 268–81.

IJsselsteijn, W.A. (2005) History of telepresence. In O. Schreer, P. Kauff and T. Sikora (eds) *3D Communication: Algorithms, Concepts and Real-time Systems in Human Centred Communication* (pp. 7–22). Chichester: John Wiley & Sons.

Innes, C. (2003) Theory, practice and modern drama. Available from: *http://moderndrama.ca/crc/resources/essays/theories_of_drama.php*.

Ippolito, J. (1999) Is cyberspace really a space? *Artbyte* 5: 16–17.

Järvinen, A., Heliö, S. and Mäyrä, F. (2002) Communication and community in digital entertainment services: prestudy research report. Tampere: University of Tampere Hypermedia Laboratory. Available from: *http://tampub.uta.fi/tup/951-44-5432-4.pdf*.

Jenkins, H. (2011) Transmedia 202: further reflections. Confessions of an Aca-fan: the official weblog of Henry Jenkins, August. Available from: *http://henryjenkins.org/2011/08/defining_transmedia_further_re.html*.

Jones, M. (2008) Featured 3D resource: Southhampton in 1454: a three-dimensional model of the medieval town, *3DVisA Bulletin* 4 (March). Available from: *http://3dvisa.cch.kcl.ac.uk/paper_jones.html*.

Joslin, C., Di Giacomo, T. and Magnenat-Thalmann, N. (2004) Collaborative virtual environments: from birth to standardization, *Communications Magazine, IEEE* 42(4): 28–33.

Kafka, F. (1915) *The Metamorphosis*, translated by S. Corngold (1972). New York: Bantam Classics Edition, 1981.

Kalay. Y.E. (2004) Virtual learning environments, *ITcon* 9: 195 207.

Kalay, Y.E. (2006) The impact of information technology on design methods, products and practices, *Design Studies* 27: 357–80.

Kaye, N. (2000) *Site-Specific Art: Performance, Place and Documentation*. London: Routledge.

Kehrwald, B. (2008) Understanding social presence in text-based online learning environments, *Distance Education* 29(1): 89–106.

King, R. and Fouts, J. (2009) Digital diplomacy: understanding Islam through virtual worlds. Carnegie Council. Available from: *http://www.carnegiecouncil.org/publications/articles_papers_reports/0014.html/_res/id=sa_File1/PolicyPaper_DigitalDiplomacy.pdf*.

Kirriemuir, J. (2010) Zen and the art of avatar maintenance: a meditation on virtual worlds. Eduserv. Available from: *http://virtualworldwatch.net/wordpress/wp-content/uploads/2010/05/Zen.pdf*.

Kuksa, I. (2007) Scenography and new media technologies: history, educational applications and visualization techniques. Ph.D. thesis, University of Warwick.

Kuksa, I. (2008a) Virtual reality in theatre education and design practice – new developments and applications, *Art, Design and Communication in Higher Education* 7(2): 73–89.

Kuksa, I. (2008b) The Set-SPECTRUM Project – a new educational approach to studying theatre history and scene design, *Theatre Design and Technology* 44(4): 49–57.

Kuksa, I. and Childs, M. (2010) But a walking shadow: designing, performing and learning on the virtual stage, *Learning Media and Technology* 35(3): 275–91.

Kuksa, I. and Tuck, D. (2011) 'Breaking the glass': preserving social history in virtual environments, *International Journal of Arts and Technology* 4(4): 392–407.

Lombard, M. and Ditton, T. (1997) At the heart of it all: the concept of presence, *Journal of Computer Mediated Communication* 3(2). Available from: *http://onlinelibrary.wiley.com/doi/10.1111/j.1083-6101.1997.tb00072.x/full.*

Machado, I., Paiva, A. and Prada, R. (2001) *Is the Wolf Angry Or ... Just Hungry? Inspecting, Modifying and Sharing Characters' Minds.* Course materials for online workshop on narrative learning environments, Kaleidoscope Virtual Doctoral School, University of Genoa, October–December 2006.

Markoff, J. (2006) Entrepreneurs see a web guided by common sense, *The New York Times* 12 November. Available from: *http://www.nytimes.com/2006/11/12/business/12web.html?pagewanted=all&_r=0.*

Masterman, E. (2008) Activity theory and the design of pedagogic planning tools. In L. Lockyer, S. Bennett, S. Agostinho and B. Harper (eds) *Handbook of Research on Learning Design and Learning Objects: Issues, Applications and Technologies* (pp. 209–27) (two volumes). Hershey, PA: IGI Global.

McAuley, G. (2000) *Space in Performance: Making Meaning in the Theatre*, 2nd edition. Ann Arbor, MI: University of Michigan Press.

McGeoch, K. and Hughes, J. (2009) Digital storytelling and drama: language, image and empathy. In M. Anderson, J. Caroll and D. Cameron (eds) *Drama Education with Digital Technology* (pp. 113–28). London: Continuum.

McKnight, J.C. (2011) Games & culture: why the magic circle is ass, *Aporia* (weblog 5 September). Available from: *http://www.johncartermcknight.com/blog/?p=1116*>.

McKnight, J.C. (2012) Mittens and the magic circle, *Aporia* (weblog 28 March). Available from: *http://www.johncartermcknight.com/blog/?p=1720*>.

McLuhan, M. (1964) *Understanding Media: The Extensions of Man.* New York: McGraw Hill.

Merchant, G., Gillen, J., Marsh, J. and Davies, J. (2013) *Virtual Literacies: Interactive Spaces for Children and Young People*. New York: Routledge.

Message, K. (2009) Museum studies: borderwork, genealogy, revolution, *Museum and Society* 7(2): 125–32.

Meyer, M. (1995) Dramatic narrative in virtual reality. In F. Biocca and M.R. Levy (eds) *Communication in the Age of Virtual Reality* (pp. 219–58). Hillsdale, NJ: Lawrence Erlbaum Associates.

Milgram, P. and Drascic, D. (1997) Perceptual effects in aligning virtual and real objects in augmented reality displays. Paper presented at the 41st Annual Meeting of Human Factors and Ergonomics Society, Albuquerque, New Mexico, September.

Minsky, M. (1980) Telepresence, *Omni* (June): 45–51.

Minsky, M. (2001) Postscript to 'telepresence', *Memoriam*. Available from: *http://web.media.mit.edu/~minsky/papers/Telepresence.html*.

Möntmann, N. (2009) The rise and fall of new institutionalism: perspectives on a possible future. In G. Raunig and G. Ray (eds) *Art and Contemporary Critical Practice: Reinventing Institutional Critique* (pp. 155–9). London: Mayfly Books.

Murray, D.C. and Sixsmith, J. (1999) The corporeal body in virtual reality, *Ethos* 27(3): *Body, Self, and Technology*, September: 315–43.

Murray, J.H. (1997) *Hamlet on the Holodeck: The Future of Narrative in Cyberspace*. New York: The Free Press.

Nadolny, L. and Childs, M. (in preparation) Factors for student engagement in an educational virtual world activity.

North, M.M., North, S.M. and Coble, J.R. (2002) Virtual reality therapy: an effective treatment for psychological disorders. In K.M. Stanney (ed.) *Handbook of Virtual Environments: Design, Implementation and Applications* (pp. 1065–78). Mahwah, NJ: Lawrence Erlbaum Associates.

Oldenburg, R. and Brissett, D. (1982) The third place, *Qualitative Sociology* 5(4): 265–84.

Olson, K.K. (2000) Cyberspace as place and the limits of metaphor, *Convergence* 11(1): 10–18.

Ondrejka, C. (2005) Changing realities: user creation, communication, and innovation in digital worlds. Available from: *http://ssrn.com/abstract=799468* or *http://dx.doi.org/10.2139/ssrn.799468*.

Packer, R. and Jordan, K. (eds) (2001) *Multimedia: From Wagner to Virtual Reality*. New York: W.W. Norton & Company.

Parry, R. (2007) *Recoding the Museum: Digital Heritage and the Technologies of Change*. Oxford: Routledge.

Patel, K.K. and Vij, S.K. (2010) Spatial navigation in virtual worlds. In P.S. Sajja and R.A. Akerkar (eds) *Advanced Knowledge Based Systems: Model, Applications & Research*, volume 1 (pp. 101–25). Kolhapur, India: TMRF eBook Series.

Pavlidis, G., Koutsoudis, A., Arnaoutoglou, F., Tsioukas, V. and Chamzas, C. (2007) Methods for 3D digitization of cultural heritage, *Journal of Cultural Heritage* 8: 93–8.

Peachey, A. (2010) The third place in Second Life. In A. Peachey, J. Gillen, D. Livingstone and S. Smith-Robbins (eds) *Researching Learning in Virtual Worlds* (pp. 91–110). London: Springer.

Preston, P. and Rogers, J. (2011) Social networks, legal innovations and the 'new' music industry, *Info* 13(6): 8–19.

Pujol, L. and Champion, E. (2012) Evaluating presence in cultural heritage projects, *International Journal of Heritage Studies* 18(1): 83–102.

Reaney, M. (2000) Art in real-time: theatre and virtual reality. Seminar CIRen, 24 March 2000, University of Paris. Available from: *http://www.ciren.org/ciren/conferences/240300/index_E.html.*

Reaney, M., Unruh, D. and Hudson-Mairet, S. (2004) The edge of the illusion: a virtual reality production of *The Magic Flute*, *Theatre Design and Technology* 40(4): 10–19.

Ridgman, J. (ed.) (1998) *Boxed Sets: Television Representations of Theatre*. Luton: John Libbey Media.

Roberts, J.D. (1979) *Norman Bel Geddes: An Exhibition of Theatrical and Industrial Designs*. Austin, TX: The University of Texas Press.

Rodriguez, H. (2006) The playful and the serious: an approximation to Huizinga's *Homo Ludens, Game Studies: The International Journal of Computer Game Research* 6(1). Available from: *http://gamestudies.org/0601/articles/rodriges.*

Ryan, M. and Childs, M. (2011) Synthetic societies or pseudo realities? Debating the ethical dilemmas of Second Life. In D. Weir and N. Sultan (eds) *From Critique to Action: The Practical Ethics of the Organizational World* (pp. 254–72). Newcastle-upon-Tyne: Cambridge Scholars Press.

Sadowski, W. and Stanney, K. (2002) Presence in virtual environments. In K.M. Stanney (ed.) *Handbook of Virtual Environments: Design, Implementation and Applications* (pp. 791–808). Mahwah, NJ: Lawrence Erlbaum Associates.

Saler, M. (2012) *As If: Modern Enchantment and the Literary Prehistory of Virtual Reality*. Oxford: Oxford University Press.

Sas, C. and O'Hare, G.M.P. (2003) Presence equation: an investigation into cognitive factors underlying presence, *Presence* 12(5): 523–37.

Savin-Baden, M. (2013) Spaces in between us: a qualitative study into the impact of spatial practice when learning in Second Life, *London Review of Education* 11(1): 59–75.

Schechner, R. (2006) *Performance Studies: An Introduction*, 2nd edition. London: Routledge.

Schroeder, R. (ed.) (2002) *The Social Life of Avatars*. London: Springer.

Sculley, J. (1987) *Odyssey: Pepsi to Apple: A Journey of Adventure, Ideas, and the Future*. New York: Harper & Row.

Shaffer, D.W. (2006) *How Computer Games Help Children Learn*. New York: Macmillan.

Sheridan, T. (1992) Musings on telepresence and virtual presence, *Presence: Teleoperators and Virtual Environments* 1(1): 120–6.

Smith, A.D. (2007) The flesh of perception: Merleau-Ponty and Husserl. In T. Baldwin (ed.) *Reading Merleau-Ponty: On Phenomenology of Perception* (pp. 1–22). London: Routledge.

Smith, K. (2002) Translation as secondary communication. The relevance theory perspective of Ernst-August Gutt, *Acta Theologica Supplementum* 2: 107–16.

Smith, L. (2006) *The Uses of Heritage*. London: Routledge.

Spivack, N. (2006) Web 3.0: the third generation Web is coming. Special report for the Lifeboat Foundation. Available from: *http://lifeboat.com/ex/web.3.0*.

Steinkuehler, C.A. (2005) The new third place: massively multiplayer online gaming in American youth culture, *Journal of Research in Teacher Education* 3: 16–33.

Steuer, J. (1995) Defining virtual reality: dimensions determining telepresence. In F. Biocca and M.R. Levy (eds) *Communication in the Age of Virtual Reality* (pp. 33–56). Mahwah, NJ: Lawrence Erlbaum Associates.

Steventon, G., Grove, P. and Childs, M. (2008) Shared spaces and 'safe' urban jungles: juggling pedagogical goals and student needs and expectations in a Second Life virtual community. In *Proceedings of the ASCILITE Conference* (pp. 975–82), Melbourne, Deakin University.

Story, M.F. (1998) Maximizing usability: the principles of universal design, *The Assistive Technology Journal* 10: 4–12.

Styliani, S., Fotis, L., Kostas, K. and Petros, P. (2009) Virtual museums: a survey and some issues for consideration, *Journal of Cultural Heritage* 10: 520–8.

Suits, B. (2005) *The Grasshopper: Games, Life and Utopia*. Peterborough, ON: Broadview Press.

Timmis, S. (2011) Constant companions: instant messaging conversations as sustainable supportive study structures amongst undergraduate peers, *Computers & Education* 59: 3–18.

Towell, J. and Towell, E. (1997) Presence in text-based networked virtual environments or 'MUDS', *Presence* 6(5): 590–5.

Tuck, D., Kuksa, I. and Guest, R. (2009) Narrating the past project: navigating around the story space. In *Proceedings of ICERI2009* (pp. 1378–83).

Turkle, S. (1995) *Life on the Screen: Identity in the Age of the Internet*. New York: Simon & Schuster.

Turner, V. (1969) *The Ritual Process: Structure and Anti-Structure*. Chicago, IL: Aldine Publishing.

UNESCO (2005) *Information and Communication Technologies in Schools – A Handbook for teachers*. Available from: *http://unesdoc.unesco.org/images/0013/001390/139028e.pdf*.

van Haperen, K. (2001) The value of simulation exercises for emergency management in the United Kingdom, *Risk Management* 3(4): 35–50.

Velmans, M (1998) Physical, psychological and virtual realities. In J. Wood (ed.) *The Virtual Embodied* (pp. 45–60). London: Routledge.

Wagner, R. (1849) *The Revolution*. Printed in *Volksblätter*, 14. Dresden, 8 April 1849.

Wenger, E. (1998) *Communities of Practice: Learning, Meaning and Identity*. Cambridge: Cambridge University Press.

Wenger, E. (2000) Communities of practice and social learning systems, *Organization* 7(2): 225–46.

White, D. (2013) Across the divide: tackling digital exclusion in Glasgow. Report for Carnegie UK Trust. Available from: *http://www.carnegieuktrust.org.uk/CMSPages/GetFile.aspx?guid=50915777-d807-4561-9527-b45aee5d5014*.

White, M. (2001) Visual pleasure in textual places. In E. Green and A. Adam (eds) *Virtual Gender: Technology, Consumption and Identity* (pp. 124–49). London: Routledge.

Whitehead, C. (2007) Establishing the manifesto: art histories in the nineteenth-century museum. In S.J. Knell, S. MacLeod and S. Watson (eds) *Museum Revolutions: How Museums Change and Are Changed* (pp. 45–60). London and New York: Routledge.

Whitworth, B. (2010) The emergence of the physical world from information processing, *Quantum Biosystems* 2(1): 221–49.

Willats, S. (2012) *Artwork as Social Model: A Manual of Questions and Propositions*. Sheffield: RGAP.

Willemen, P. (2002) Reflections on digital imagery: of mice and men. In M. Rieser and A. Zapp (eds) *New Screen Media: Cinema/Art/Narrative* (pp. 14–26). London: British Film Institute.

Witcomb, A. (2007) The materiality of virtual technologies: a new approach to thinking about the impact of multimedia in museums. In F. Cameron and S. Kenderdine (eds) *Theorizing Digital Cultural Heritage: A Critical Discourse* (pp. 35–48). Cambridge, MA: MIT Press.

Wu, Y. and Xu, R. (2011) The application of Chomsky's syntactic theory in translation study, *Journal of Language Teaching and Research* 2(2): 396–9.

Wunderer, M. (2002) Presence in front of the fourth wall of cyberspace. In S.A. Schrum (ed.) *Theatre in Cyberspace: Issues of Teaching, Acting, and Directing* (pp. 203–20). New York: Peter Lang.

Zellner, D. (1999) Definitions and directions of the theatre. In S.A. Schrum (ed.) *Theatre in Cyberspace: Issues of Teaching, Acting, and Directing* (pp. 19–29). New York: Peter Lang.

Zhao, S. (2003) Toward a taxonomy of copresence, *Presence* 12(5): 445–55.

Index

Lightning Source UK Ltd.
Milton Keynes UK
UKOW03f0402040714

234559UK00006B/188/P

9 781843 347408